What people are saying about

Dynamic Interactive Astrology

Lyn Birkbeck makes astrology accessible. He reminds me of an old science teacher who once told me that if you learn to understand the basic structures, then you never have to worry about memorising anything as you can work it out for yourself. Lyn has a genius touch for equipping you with simple tools to examine a chart, which in turn allow you to unlock a whole new universe of insights and understandings.
Karen Sealey (UK)

This system for understanding astrology changed my life. Dynamic Interactive Astrology made the subject remarkably easy to grasp, while providing many layers of depth for understanding myself better. The archetypes of Zodiac signs, planets and houses came alive for me, and I really liked using the keywords as catalysts for my intuition. Lyn is a brilliant and extraordinary teacher who makes the subject of astrology fun to learn and applicable to my life. Highly recommended!
Frank Kwiakowski (USA)

I have learned so much from Lyn's courses and books! Despite following many others, Lyn is my favourite astrologer. What I love the most is the depth and breadth of insight contained in just one single sentence. He distils huge concepts/paradigms down into keywords for students to link information together in a bite-sized manner, yet without losing the whole. T~ genius.
Tara Morrison (Canada)

In Lyn's accessible yet deeply knowledgeable course I learnt to experience astrology in its full complexity. But the experience itself was easy and fully enjoyable.
Steph Engert (Germany)

Dynamic Interactive Astrology is an interesting, easy to follow course and one which is fun to do. Each completed section leaves one eager to move on to find out more about the planets and their influences. It's a relevant, meaningful and inspiring course – written by an expert in his field. Lyn has a fantastic way of explaining things and takes one through this program step by step, making links with each section as he goes. I'm in awe of his knowledge, insight and understanding of astrology.
Daphne Tomkins (UK)

My husband and I studied Dynamic Interactive Astrology to learn more about ourselves, each other and how we relate. Astrology was something that I have studied and have had my chart read but I could never get my mind around understanding how it works. Lyn has created a system of instruction that is easy to understand. It is organized in a way where each lesson builds upon the previous lessons. He provides concise one word explanations for the planets, houses and other properties of the chart. Examples are given on how to work the exercises so that applying the lesson to your personal information is a snap. Words like ascendant, south node or aspects don't intimidate me anymore. Lyn removes the mystery of learning and opens the door to the mastery of self-understanding.
Karen Knight, MS, LMHC (USA)

The Dynamic Interactive Astrology method was a breakthrough for me as an amateur astrologer. I have recommended it to friends who are complete beginners and they have been thrilled to pick up astrology so quickly. It is an incredibly speedy way

to learn and get to grips with the fundamentals of astrology, i.e. the planets, the signs and houses. The method is immediately engaging and creative. You can come back to it time and again and get deeper insights.
Vivienne Rush (UK)

I found engaging with Lyn Birkbeck's Dynamic Interactive Astrology utterly fascinating, and more than that, rewarding. As an absolute novice, I found the interactive element an excellent way to embed the learning and to engage deeply with the subject matter rather than just read about it. In learning about astrology I also learned a lot about me! Highly recommended.
Derek Bain (UK)

We are in the time where we need to be cognizant of the dynamics around us. This system will give you the tools to understand and work with the dynamics, regardless of whether you are a beginner or an experienced astrologer. You will be amazed at the increased vibrancy of your interpretation of the planets.
Wayne Nicholson (Canada)

Dynamic Interactive Astrology is a must-have book for all those interested in conscious awareness and are ready for a key to unlock greater meaning. The mysteries of astrology are made simple as this book provides a plethora of keywords to associate with the planets, signs and houses of an astrological chart. And then there are easy to follow exercises that bring the reading to life. Before I knew it, I gained in depth self-knowledge from my natal chart, as well as the ability to read charts for other people.
Roz Pilling (UK)

Dynamic Interactive Astrology – Level One

Dynamic Interactive Astrology – Level One

Lyn Birkbeck

Winchester, UK
Washington, USA

JOHN HUNT PUBLISHING

First published by O-Books, 2022
O-Books is an imprint of John Hunt Publishing Ltd., 3 East St., Alresford,
Hampshire SO24 9EE, UK
office@jhpbooks.com
www.johnhuntpublishing.com
www.o-books.com

For distributor details and how to order please visit the 'Ordering' section on our website.

ISBN: 978 1 78904 623 6
978 1 78904 624 3 (ebook)
Library of Congress Control Number: 2021930559

A CIP catalogue record for this book is available from the British Library.

Design: Matthew Greenfield

UK: Printed and bound by CPI Group (UK) Ltd, Croydon, CR0 4YY
Printed in North America by CPI GPS partners

We operate a distinctive and ethical publishing philosophy in
all areas of our business, from our global network of authors to
production and worldwide distribution.

Contents

Also by this Author

The Sabian Symbols: The Astrological Oracle
ASIN: B01LYDEQW5

Encountering Dragons: An Anthology
ASIN: B00R8LR714

Understanding The Future: A Survivor's Guide to
Riding the Cosmic Wave
ISBN: 978-1905857777

Astro-Wisdom: The Knowledge, Love and
Power in your Stars
ISBN: 978-8178222431

Do It Yourself Relationship Astrology
ISBN: 978-0785824237

Do It Yourself Astrology: A User-Friendly
Guide to Your Personality
ISBN-13: 978-0785824213

The Watkins Astrology Handbook: The Practical
System of DIY Astrology
ISBN: 978-1842931677

Divine Astrology: Enlisting the Aid of the Planetary Powers
ISBN: 978-1905047031

The Instant Astrologer
ISBN: 978-1903816493

Also by this Author

The Astrological Oracle: Divining Your
Future and Resolving Your Past
ISBN: 978-0007127665

Do It Yourself Life Plan Astrology: How Planetary
Cycles Affect Your Whole Life
ISBN: 978-1862047334

Introduction

Dynamic and Descriptive

Through Exercises in which you *Profile* all the Planets and Points – which are arranged in *pairs* for reasons you will very soon discover – *Dynamic Interactive Astrology* utilizes your birth chart in an *interactive* way that directly brings to life and into consciousness your personal *dynamics*. These amount to the truth of your being which actually drives and energizes you, that which determines what kind of life you have. Through the *Dynamic Interactive Astrology* process you will also come to describe for yourself your positive personality traits, and automatically and progressively overcome your negative ones.

The first advantage here is that the method itself can be used straightaway without any prior knowledge of the complexities of astrology. This you will realize with the very first Exercise which begins after a very brief explanation of how all the Exercises work.

The second advantage is born of the fact that the *Dynamic Interactive Astrology* method automatically taps into the very essence of who and what you are by unlocking the very parts of you that comprise that essence *through engaging with and affirming your own innate self-awareness*.

The *Dynamic Interactive Astrology* process can then be used by anyone else, either with you helping them with the benefit of your own experience of *Dynamic Interactive Astrology*, or of course they can simply do it on their own. More about Interpreting Someone Else's Birth Chart is given on page 4.

It is also highly recommended that you apply *Dynamic Interactive Astrology* to Celebrities or Notable Individuals (their charts are usually available on the Internet) as this provides a very real grasp of the usage of this process.

Basic Requirements

Your Birth Chart

Prior to utilizing *Dynamic Interactive Astrology* you need to first have the Birth Chart that you wish to use. This should initially be your own, but later you will possibly be applying *Dynamic Interactive Astrology* to others (see 'Interpreting Someone Else's Birth Chart' on page 4). You will also need to be able to read *from* the Birth Chart – or at least initially be told – the various pieces of information needed for using *Dynamic Interactive Astrology*. These are as follows:

The *Signs* in which the Sun, Moon, Mercury, Venus, Mars, Jupiter, Saturn, Uranus, Neptune, Pluto, Ascendant (Rising Sign), Midheaven and Lunar Nodes are placed.

The *Houses* in which the Sun, Moon, Mercury, Venus, Mars, Jupiter, Saturn, Uranus, Neptune, Pluto and Lunar Nodes are placed.

The *Major Aspects* between the Sun, Moon, Mercury, Venus, Mars, Jupiter, Saturn, Uranus, Neptune, Pluto, Ascendant, Midheaven and Lunar Nodes. NOTE: You won't need to read off or use Aspects until *Dynamic Interactive Astrology – Level Two*.

If you do not have a Birth Chart or its information already, you may acquire it from a number of sources on the Internet.

Here is a FREE one from me:
http://www.lynbirkbeck.com/instantreports.html

As well as being free, this chart makes it easy to read off the data required for using this book. Just fill in the requested details and click **Get Free Chartwheel**. If you choose this you may also like to refer to a general explanation of the chart itself, called CHART 'A', in the Toolkit on page 278.

The Exercises

IMPORTANT!

SCAN OR PHOTOCOPY THE EXERCISES so you can use them more than once.

Use *extra paper if required* in order to complete the Exercises to your satisfaction.

The Exercises consist of **Profiling** each Planet and Point in your birth chart by compiling simple *Keyphrases* out of keywords, which are then followed by the *special questions* that tap simultaneously into your birth chart and your personality itself.

NOTE: The first few Questions are stock questions used for all Planets and Points. The Questions after these specifically correspond to the Planet or Point you are Profiling.

Initially, you obtain the keywords from the **Primary Dynamic Keywords**, and then later if you wish, from the **Keyword Clouds**. Both of these you'll find in the Toolkit beginning page 250.

Interpreting Someone Else's Birth Chart

After having applied *Dynamic Interactive Astrology* to yourself you can then go on to helping another person interpret their birth chart. *Dynamic Interactive Astrology* is a very 'clean' method as it does not involve that other person being *told* what they are like, something which is best not done other than by a professional astrologer or counsellor. So, after assisting them with the identification of the various astrological indications, as described on the previous page, by putting the Questions to them they will naturally – perhaps with some prompting from you – elicit information about the workings of their life and personality in a similar way to how you found it worked for you.

Using *Dynamic Interactive Astrology* in this way, either with yourself and another as just described, or in a group, can be very enlightening, bonding, and fun too – especially through sharing and discussing on the *Dynamic Interactive Astrology Facebook Group* at: www.facebook.com/groups/dynamicinteractiveastrology

The Sun & The Moon

The Lights

The Sun and Moon in your birth chart show what lights your way in the sense of your *conscious will* (Sun) and your *unconscious will* (Moon). Curiously though, we can often, to varying degrees, be unaware of both our conscious and unconscious wills!

Profiling these, the Lights, will make them both brighter and more positive. Profiling your Sun and Moon, especially your Sun & Moon Blend, will also make your conscious and unconscious wills operate together, making for a far more effective and harmonious life.

The Sun is the *life force*. It is the *creator* of everything in this Solar System. In your birth chart therefore, it represents your *spirit*, your *heart*, and what is of *central importance* to you. The Sun is what is actually giving you *vitality*. The Sun portrays the nature of your *will* and *purpose* in life. Negatively it is *conceit* and *egotism*. The Sun is the center of your being, and all other planetary influences are arranged around it.

The Moon reflects the light of the Sun, your conscious will, and as such it symbolizes your *feeling responses* and your *reactions* to life around you. In *childhood*, before your will had started to become conscious, the fulfilling of your *security needs* made you totally dependent on others, especially your *mother*. Consequently, much of your personality became conditioned by the *habits* and *biases* of her, and of *your family, race, class, etc*. These influences relate to your *needs* and *survival instincts, sympathy, receptivity*, and *sense of belonging* and *inner support*. But the negative expressions of the Moon, like *clannishness, fear of the unknown, insecurity,* and *defensiveness*, need to be brought into conscious awareness and sorted out. What is *safe* and *familiar* is fine just so long as it is not just a case of *clinging* to *the past* and eclipsing your individuality.

REMINDER! SCAN OR PHOTOCOPY THE EXERCISES so you can use them more than once. Use *extra paper if required* in order to complete the Exercises to your satisfaction.

Exercise 1 - Profiling Sun

1. In the table below headed ☉ *PROFILING SUN*, **after** the *Example*, insert the position of the SUN by SIGN and HOUSE (as given in your chart) in the third row in the relevant columns. *Enter name top-right.*

    2. From the **Primary Dynamic Keywords** on page 251. freely select **one** keyword each for SUN, SIGN and HOUSE and then insert them in the fourth row in the appropriate columns as in the *Example* below. You now have your Sun Keyphrase on the fourth row, which for our Example of Oprah Winfrey is: "(My) Purpose (is) to Liberate Self-Expression."

Example		*Oprah Winfrey*
PLANET	SIGN	HOUSE
SUN	*Aquarius*	*5th*
Purpose	*To Liberate*	*Self-Expression*

☉ *PROFILING SUN:*		
PLANET	SIGN	HOUSE
SUN		

3. When you have done the above, answer the following Sun Questions. While answering these questions you may also refer to the appropriate **Keyword Clouds** – which are found in the Toolkit on page 258 – if you feel the need to jog your mind, enhance meaning or stimulate your imagination.

Sun Questions

☺ *If you cannot answer any question come back to it later.*

a) Record or write down freely the feelings, thoughts and impressions that you experience on reading and pondering your Sun Keyphrase.

b) What character traits would you say are evidence or expressions of your Sun Keyphrase?

c) What events, achievements or situations, if any, would you say are a testament to your being true to your Sun Keyphrase?

d) What events, situations or feelings, if any, would you say are a testament to your NOT being true to your Sun Keyphrase? How could you move on through or out of such situations in order to embody or realize your Sun Keyphrase?

e) What does all this tell you about your ego as a healthy sense of self? Consider how you feel about your own significance.

f) What does all this tell you about your ego as a *false* sense of self? Consider, in the light of your Sun Keyphrase, how you feel about your own authenticity.

g) How do you think or feel your father figures in the expression or experience of your Sun Keyphrase or Profile?

h) The energy and progress that you and your life has available to it are determined by the degree to which you are focused on and giving positive expression to your Sun Keyphrase. To what degree do you think you are doing so, and what can be done, if necessary, to increase that degree? At the same time, consider what issues or circumstances might be getting in the way of you accomplishing this. This may be something that you would like to share and discuss on the *Dynamic Interactive Astrology Facebook Group* at:

www.facebook.com/groups/dynamicinteractiveastrology

i) If you were to see yourself as the star in the film that is your own life, how, in the context of your Sun Keyphrase, would you describe such a character and role in dramatic terms? And, possibly more importantly, what would be the *narrative arc (the various Scenes and Acts of your life story)* – and the point you have got to in your story so far?

j) Make a summing up statement concerning all of the above. Doing this will reveal to you how through using *Dynamic Interactive Astrology* you are becoming not only versed in astrology, but becoming more aware of yourself as a unique individual. Feel free to share parts of your Summary Statement in the *Dynamic Interactive Astrology Facebook Group* at: www.facebook.com/groups/dynamicinteractiveastrology

Additional Sun Exercises

It is recommended that having completed the above, you do it all again, now or later, choosing another set of Dynamic Keywords to make a different Sun Sign and House Keyphrase. You can also refer to the relevant **Keyword Clouds** on page 258 for extra, sometimes more advanced, keywords.

This gives you another slant on the chart/person's dynamics and characteristics.

You can repeat this with alternative keywords as many times as you like or see fit.

Exercise 2 - Profiling Moon

1. In the table below headed ☽ *PROFILING MOON*, **after** the *Example*, insert the position of the MOON by SIGN and HOUSE (as given in your chart) in the third row in the relevant columns. *Enter name top-right.*

    2. From the **Primary Dynamic Keywords** on page 253 freely select **one** keyword each for MOON, SIGN and HOUSE and then insert them in the fourth row in the appropriate columns as in the *Example* below. You now have your Moon Keyphrase on the fourth row, which for our Example of Oprah Winfrey is: "(I have an) Instinct to Develop Foundations."

Example		*Oprah Winfrey*
PLANET	SIGN	HOUSE
MOON	*Sagittarius*	*4th*
Instinct	*To Develop*	*Foundations*

☽ *PROFILING MOON:*		
PLANET	SIGN	HOUSE
MOON		

3. When you have done the above, answer the following questions. While answering these questions you may also refer to the appropriate **Keyword Clouds** – which are found in the Toolkit on page 259 – if you feel the need to jog your mind, enhance meaning or stimulate your imagination.

Moon Questions

☺ *If you cannot answer any question come back to it later.*

a) Record or write down freely the feelings, thoughts and impressions that you experience on reading and pondering your Moon Keyphrase.

b) What character traits would you say you possess that are evidence or expressions of your Moon Keyphrase?

c) What events, achievements or situations, if any, would you say are a testament to your being true to your Moon Keyphrase?

d) What events, situations or feelings, if any, would you say are a testament to your NOT being true to your Moon Keyphrase? How could you move on through or out of such situations in order to embody or realize your Moon Keyphrase?

e) What does all this tell you about your good and bad habits? In other words, what habits serve the positive expression of your Moon Keyphrase, and your life generally, and which ones don't?

f) How do you think or feel your mother figures in the expression or experience of your Moon Keyphrase or Profile?

g) In what ways does being true to your Moon Keyphrase bring comfort, safety and security into your life?

h) How do you feel the nature of your Moon Keyphrase or Profile describes or affects your reactions and responses to life, particularly with regard to the House position keyword?

i) Do you feel the expression and qualities of your Moon Keyphrase come naturally to you, like they were there from early on in life, in your childhood? If so, in what way? And was there ever a time when they ceased to come naturally – partially or completely?

j) Have you noticed that the expression of your Moon Keyphrase goes through phases, ups and downs, and is very susceptible to your moods? Comment.

k) Make a summing up statement concerning all of the above. Doing this will reveal to you how through using *Dynamic Interactive Astrology* you are becoming not only versed in astrology, but becoming more aware of yourself as a unique individual. Feel free to share parts of your Summary Statement in the *Dynamic Interactive Astrology Facebook Group* at: www.facebook.com/groups/dynamicinteractiveastrology

Additional Moon Exercises

It is recommended that having completed the above, you do it all again, now or later, choosing another set of Dynamic Keywords to make a different Moon Sign and House Keyphrase. You can repeat this with alternative keywords as many times as you like or see fit. You can also refer to the relevant **Keyword Clouds** on page 259 for extra, sometimes more advanced keywords.

This gives you another slant on the chart/person's dynamics and characteristics.

Exercise 3 - Profiling Sun & Moon Blend

There is something in astrology called the Core Blend which is the combining of the energies or influences of the Sun, Moon and Ascendant in an individual's birth chart. In this exercise you will discover how first blending your Sun and Moon will reveal to you the engine that powers your very existence. We will add your Ascendant to this later on page 213 under Completing Core Blend.

The Sun is the conscious 'you', and the Moon is the unconscious 'you' which thereby acts as a *feed* to the Sun. Think *fuel* (Moon) and *fire* (Sun).

1. In the table below headed ☉☽ *PROFILING SUN & MOON BLEND*, **after** the *Example* – again using Oprah Winfrey, with her Moon in Sagittarius in the 4th House, and now too her Sun in Aquarius in the 5th House with Primary Keywords making her Sun Keyphrase – insert your Moon Keyphrase (that you Profiled in Exercise 2) in the third row of the first column, and your Sun Keyphrase (Profiled in Exercise 1) in the third row of the third column. ***Enter name top-right.*** With the Action Keyphrase, 'Feeds or Drives', in the middle, together we could say this whole third row is now one summing up or statement of your Sun & Moon Blend. Arriving at our Sun & Moon Blend like this, we can appreciate how our chart maps out this core energy that powers us. Now note your Spontaneous Reaction to this summing up or statement and enter it in the space provided beneath this statement. Then, if you like, jot down any Further Impressions in the space provided. Finally you can let this sit with you for as long as you want and see what else arises.

Example PROFILING SUN & MOON BLEND		*Oprah Winfrey*
MOON KEYPHRASE	ACTION	SUN KEYPHRASE
Instinct to Develop Foundations	Feeds or Drives	*Purpose to Liberate Self-Expression*

Spontaneous Reaction:

Possibly (we can only surmise as such a reaction is very personal) this feels like something really important and significant falling into place inside of her.

Further Impressions:

It could be said, drawing from the Moon and Sagittarius Keyword Clouds, that her Childhood (which was very unhappy) Furthered her Purpose to Liberate Self-Expression.

☉☽ PROFILING SUN & MOON BLEND:

MOON KEYPHRASE	ACTION	SUN KEYPHRASE
	Feeds or Drives	

Spontaneous Reaction:

Further Impressions:

2. Your Sun & Moon Blend will not only show you how your Needs feed your Purpose, but also how your Purpose *satisfies* your Needs. This is a *beautiful symbiosis*: the Sun shines upon the Moon as the Moon reflects the light of the Sun.

So, to this end, in the table below headed ☉☽ *REVERSE PROFILING SUN & MOON BLEND*, **after** the *Example*, insert your Sun Keyphrase in the third row in the first column (possibly, as in this *Example, reselecting* the Sun keyword from the Sun Keyword Cloud on page 258), and insert your Moon Keyphrase in the third row in the third column (same keywords used here but reselect if you wish). *Enter name top-right.* It will now, with the given Action phrase, read as a statement (see *Example*). Again, in the fourth row, first note your Spontaneous Reaction to this statement. Then, if you like, jot down any further impressions that you get from it in the fifth row against Further Impressions. Finally you can let this sit with you for as long as you want and see what else arises.

Example REVERSE PROFILING SUN & MOON BLEND: **Oprah Winfrey**		
SUN KEYPHRASE	ACTION	MOON KEYPHRASE
Life-Force to Liberate Self-Expression	Vitalizes or Shines upon and Satisfies	*Need to Develop Foundations*
Spontaneous Reaction: *Possibly (we can only surmise as such a reaction is very personal) a sense of satisfaction and accomplishment that encourages her to carry on indefinitely with her good works.*		
Further Impressions: *She has got on a roll here - big time!*		

☉☽ *REVERSE PROFILING SUN & MOON BLEND:*

SUN KEYPHRASE	ACTION	MOON KEYPHRASE
	Vitalizes or Shines upon and Satisfies	

Spontaneous Reaction:

Further Impressions:

You can see how all of this really *is* the engine that powers your very existence, like breathing in and breathing out! As ever, feel free to let your intuition and imagination play with the keywords and Keyphrases, and draw what inferences naturally and spontaneously arise from doing so.

As demonstrated above, bear in mind that you may need to choose some new keywords, possibly drawn from the Clouds, and compose a new Keyphrase or new Keyphrases, in order to make the Blend.

A Note on Reincarnation

One way of seeing the Sun and Moon as a dynamic whole is to consider the Moon as symbolic of the Sun in your last life, while the Sun *is* your present life. So if, for example, you have a Leo Moon in this life then you could have had a Leo Sun in your last.

You don't have to believe in reincarnation to accept this for it can be viewed purely as a metaphor.

In other words, whereas the Sun is the conscious 'you' in this life, the Moon is the unconscious 'you' from your last life and thereby acts as a *feed* to the Sun. Again, think *fuel* (Moon) and *fire* (Sun).

Mercury & Uranus

The Links

The plot thickens! Having covered The Sun & the Moon – *The Lights*, we now install *The Links*.

The *Links* are basically about Communication on a *mental* level. Mercury is the *personal or lower mind*, or *intellect, deduction, perception and connectedness (also neurologically speaking)*, while Uranus is the higher octave to Mercury's lower octave, that is, *the impersonal or universal mind*, or *intuition as meaning a sense of the truth as seen from a higher perspective*. So, Mercury, being the lower octave here, is a matter of personal perception; Uranus is the naked and untarnished truth, free of personal bias or interpretation.

It will be found that the Profiling of this, and the other planetary pairs, is rather like tuning an instrument. The lower octave resonates with the higher octave thereby properly attuning you to these planetary energies.

In the case of Uranus and Mercury, one product of this attunement could be not only you being more able to intuit the truth about something or someone, but also being able to verbalize it appropriately – which may mean *not* verbalizing it! An acute example of this is people who suffer from autism or Tourette's syndrome; they are plugged into the universal mind (truth) but cannot control too well how they express it. Yet at the same time they can be quite brilliant at playing an instrument or plucking complex facts out of thin air. They also sometimes suffer from nervous tics, a physical Mercurial symptom of resisting Uranus, as is any form of spasm or mistiming.

So with Profiling Mercury and Uranus, this is like one communications system automatically linking up to the other – like a phone or some other device linking up to the Internet. Be aware though, that there can be cross-talk between any planetary pair, something which we will explore with Aspects in *Dynamic Interactive Astrology – Level Two.*

A very simple way in which you may appreciate how *The Links* are linked themselves could be summed up in the phrase: "Freedom of Speech" – in more senses than might at first be evident.

So you may now begin by Profiling MERCURY and then proceed when ready to Profiling URANUS as you did with the Sun and Moon.

The Links being what they are, you may find it advantageous to Profile both before you finalize either one of them. This is because you may find how the Profiling of the one affects your Profiling of the other. This means that you may find that you need to edit what you have done for Mercury after insights gained while Profiling Uranus – and vice versa.

REMINDER! SCAN OR PHOTOCOPY THE EXERCISES so you can use them more than once. Use *extra paper if required* in order to complete the Exercises to your satisfaction.

Exercise 4 - Profiling Mercury

1. In the table below headed ☿ *PROFILING MERCURY*, following the *Example*, insert the position of MERCURY by SIGN and HOUSE (as given in your chart) in the third row in the relevant columns. *Enter name top-right.*

2. From the **Primary Dynamic Keywords** on page 251, freely select **one** keyword each for MERCURY, SIGN and HOUSE and then insert them in the fourth row in the appropriate columns as in the *Example* below. You now have your Mercury Keyphrase on the fourth row, which for our Example of Sir Winston Churchill is: "(I am) Communicating (in order) to Empower (much needed) Resources."

Example		*Sir Winston Churchill*
PLANET	SIGN	HOUSE
MERCURY	*Scorpio*	*2nd*
Communicating	*To Empower*	*Resources*

Important Note: Because Mercury is so close to the Sun, and closer to the Sun than the Earth is, it is never more than one Sign away *from* the Sun. This means that it is often placed in the same Sign and/or House as the Sun.

If such is the case then this simply stresses or enhances whatever your Sun Keyphrase is saying but with the emphasis on your mental and perceptual take on what that Keyphrase is revealing. And you can if you wish separate out the Living (Sun) from the Thinking (Mercury) by choosing keywords for the Sign and House of Mercury that are significantly different from your Sun's Sign and House keywords.

☿ *PROFILING MERCURY:*		
PLANET	SIGN	HOUSE
MERCURY		

3. When you have done the above, answer the following questions. While doing so you may refer to the appropriate **Keyword Clouds** – which are found in the Toolkit on page 260 if you feel the need to jog your mind, enhance meaning or stimulate your imagination.

Keyword Clouds also broaden your knowledge of astrological symbolism and correspondences generally.

Mercury Questions

☺ *If you cannot answer any question come back to it later.*

a) Record or write down freely the feelings, thoughts and impressions that you experience on reading and pondering your Mercury Keyphrase.

b) What character traits would you say were evidence or expressions of your Mercury Keyphrase? Comment on what this implies.

c) What events, achievements or situations, particularly in the field of your working life, would you say are a testament to your being true to your Mercury Keyphrase?

d) What does all this tell you about the ways you perceive life, especially in terms of how these perceptions serve you by making your life more coherent, informed and in touch with what you need to connect with or communicate?

e) In the light of the saying: "The mind makes a good servant but a poor master", what does your Mercury Keyphrase tell you about the ways you think or perceive life in terms of how such thinking and perceptions ill-serve you by making you feel disconnected or anxious, or give you trouble communicating or formulating what you wish to say? How could you alter these perceptions (with new keywords possibly) to remedy any such negative situations?

f) As Mercury rules brothers and sisters (they have a lot to do with how we communicate and perceive when young), how do you think or feel your siblings, or lack of them, have influenced the expression or experience of your Mercury Keyphrase or Profile?

g) What does your Mercury Keyphrase tell you about the nature of your work, and the way that you work?

h) Try looking at the Mercury Keyphrases for a few people you know (most easily done in the *Dynamic Interactive Astrology Facebook Group* at: www.facebook.com/groups/dynamicinteractiveastrology) in order to gain an idea of how they perceive and mentally process reality in ways different to yours, thereby posing the further question: "What *is* reality?" Also note how some Mercury positions are evidently left-brain (rational) types of Mercury, and others right-brain (intuitive) types.

i) One of the keywords that you'll find in the Mercury Keyword Cloud is 'Wit'. This is an important dimension of this Planet of thoughts, words and reason because Mercury is smart enough to know that there is an illusion or joke running through life and the way we perceive it. So, from your Mercury Keyphrase can you perceive something funny or absurd about it? If not, make up a new Keyphrase that does make you laugh, if only quietly to yourself. This is important because Mercury's logic and factuality can get too serious by half, and thereby miss the point and cause anxiety.

j) Make a summing up statement concerning all of the above. Doing this will reveal to you how through using *Dynamic Interactive Astrology* you are becoming not only versed in astrology, but becoming more aware of yourself as a unique individual. Feel free to share parts of your Summary Statement in the *Dynamic Interactive Astrology Facebook Group* at: www.facebook.com/groups/dynamicinteractiveastrology

Additional Mercury Exercises

It is recommended that having completed the above, you do it all again, now or later, choosing another set of Dynamic Keywords to make a different Mercury, Sign and House Keyphrase.

This gives you another slant on the chart/person's dynamics and characteristics.

You can repeat this with alternative keywords as many times as you like or see fit. You can also refer to the relevant Keyword Clouds on page 260 for extra, sometimes more advanced, keywords.

Exercise 5 - Profiling Uranus

1. In the table below headed ♅ *PROFILING URANUS,* **after** the *Example*, insert the position of URANUS by SIGN and HOUSE (as given in your chart) in the third row in the relevant columns. *Enter name top-right.*

2. From the **Primary Dynamic Keywords** on page 253 freely select **one** keyword each for URANUS, SIGN and HOUSE and then insert them in the fourth row in the appropriate columns as in the *Example* below. You now have your Uranus Keyphrase on the fourth row, which for our Example of Aleister Crowley can be rephrased as: "I Awaken with my Dramatic Presence."

Example	*Aleister Crowley (notorious magician)*	
PLANET	SIGN	HOUSE
URANUS	*Leo*	*1st*
Awakening	*To Dramatize*	*(type of) Presence*

♅ *PROFILING URANUS:*		
PLANET	SIGN	HOUSE
URANUS		

3. When you have done the above, answer the following questions. While doing so you may refer to the appropriate **Keyword Clouds** if you feel the need to jog your mind, enhance meaning, stimulate your imagination, or simply find the words that fit. Keyword Clouds also broaden your knowledge of astrological symbolism and correspondences generally.

Uranus Questions

☺ *If you cannot answer any question come back to it later.*

a) Record or write down freely the feelings, thoughts and impressions that you experience on reading and pondering your Uranus Keyphrase.

b) What character traits would you say were evidence or expressions of your Uranus Keyphrase?

c) What events, situations or feelings, if any, would you say are a testament to your being true to your Uranus Keyphrase?

d) What events, feelings or situations, if any, would you say are a testament to your NOT being true to your Uranus Keyphrase? How could you move on through or out of such situations in order to embody or realize your Uranus Keyphrase?

e) What does all this tell you about how your personality has changed, evolved and become truer to itself (as in Jung's *individuation* process) in your life so far?

f) As the Planet of Intuition (as a sense of the Truth) it could also be described as your *Auto-Pilot,* the part of you that just *knows* where you are truly supposed to be going and how you are going to get there. In the context of your Keyphrase, how could you see this as evidence of your Auto-Pilot in action? Invent another Keyphrase to reveal this, if necessary.

g) Unless you have already done so in answer to an earlier question, now take your Keyphrase and run with it. This means you start with the Keyphrase and then write (or better still, speak into a recorder) *automatically* with absolutely no pauses for considering whether what you are saying is 'right' or not.

This exercise is in aid of revealing something about yourself that your rational mind may have managed to hide or edit out, and/or loosening up your intuition. Uranus governs all forms of oracular and divinatory devices – astrology, tarot, etc. – and the Uranian ability to freely associate, unimpeded by rational considerations, is crucial. Uranus, like The Fool in the Tarot, steps into the Unknown with no expectations. Comment on this before and/or after doing this exercise.

h) This isn't exactly something you can do right now – although in typical Uranian fashion it might well be! – but an actual Uranus exercise to try out when you have the opportunity or mind to do so.

As the Planet of Intuition in being a sense of the Truth, whenever presented with something that requires that you are in the possession of the truth concerning it, do the following.

First of all prime your mind to be ready for such an occasion when it arises. Then when it does occur, have the presence of mind to observe the *very first thing, answer, impression, notion, etc.* that jumps into your mind. This will be happening at lightning speed and you could miss it. And if you do miss it, then your logical, sensible, rational, clever or socially acceptable answer or idea (Mercury) pops up, thinking that it was first to arrive in your mind – and therefore the right answer, but very possibly not!

Also, because Uranus is the Planet of Truth, we can be programmed to suppress it as we have been led to believe that the truth hurts. It may well do, but in truth, it also makes you free! Comment.

i) Make a summing up statement concerning all of the above. Doing this will reveal to you how through using *Dynamic Interactive Astrology* you are becoming not only versed in astrology, but becoming more aware of yourself as a unique individual. Feel free to share parts of your Summary Statement in the *Dynamic Interactive Astrology Facebook Group* at: www.facebook.com/groups/dynamicinteractiveastrology

Additional Uranus Exercises

It is recommended that having completed the above, you do it all again, now or later, choosing another set of Dynamic Keywords to make a different Uranus, Sign and House Keyphrase.

This gives you another slant on the chart/person's dynamics and characteristics.

You can repeat this with alternative keywords as many times as you like or see fit. You can also refer to the relevant Keyword Clouds for extra, sometimes more intermediate or advanced keywords.

Exercise 6 - Profiling Mercury & Uranus Talk

Attuning your Intellect and Intuition to one another.

This is an exercise that serves to bring into communication two different types of communication or mental modality: intellect and intuition. This is in aid of enabling you to think and intuit better by upgrading other areas of communication, internally and externally. This, in turn, improves your ability to read a birth chart and convey what it is saying – what is called 'getting the chart to talk'.

Some people have spontaneously found ways of linking the two Links, rather like we did with the Sun and Moon Blend. This also enhances your 'linkage' and is achieved by simply finding a way to connect your Mercury and Uranus Keyphrases with a few more words in between.

Here, as an Example, is what someone wrote doing this Exercise:

Mercury in Scorpio in the 4th House = 'contacting authentic security'; with Uranus in Virgo in the 2nd House = 'awakening to improve self-worth/talents'. Uranus supports the deepening of my inner life by strengthening my sense of self and providing ways to express it through my talents (to be discovered at a later date). My linking of the two is: 'Contacting my authentic security will awaken the energy to improve my self-worth and talents.'

Here, however, the aim is to bring Mercury and Uranus into some kind of dialogue. It helps to think of Mercury as your personal mind or intellect or computer/phone, and of Uranus as the Universal Mind or the Internet.

Here's how to set up the dialogue using the astrological symbols and their keywords.

1. Initially 'prime' your mind by having a good look at both the Mercury and Uranus Clouds on pages 260 and 265. This will make you more *conversant* with their meaning and facilitate the dialogue. To accomplish this it is very advisable to do this

exercise all in one sitting.

2. In the table below headed ☿ ♅ *PROFILING MERCURY & URANUS TALK*, following the *Example,* insert the position of MERCURY by SIGN and HOUSE (as given in your chart) in the third row in the relevant columns. *Enter name top-right.* See *Example* below.

3. From the **Primary Dynamic Keywords**, freely select **one** keyword each for MERCURY, SIGN and HOUSE and then insert them in the fourth row in the appropriate columns as in the *Example* below. If you wish, you may use the same keywords as you used before in Exercise 4. Or you may use keywords found in the Mercury Cloud on page 260.

4. Now, in the *same* table below headed ☿ ♅ *PROFILING MERCURY & URANUS TALK*, following the *Example* below, insert the position of the URANUS by SIGN and HOUSE (as given in your chart) in the fifth row in the relevant columns.

5. From the **Primary Dynamic Keywords**, freely select **one** keyword each for URANUS, SIGN and HOUSE and then insert them in the sixth row in the appropriate columns, as in the *Example* below. Note: Again, if you wish, you may use the same keywords as you used before in Exercise 5. Or you may use keywords found in the Uranus Cloud on page 265.

6. Now respond to the questions that follow in the following rows of the table (starting with 'Comment on the Combination', that is, how you see these two Keyphrases side by side, on how they combine). See *Example.*

Example PROFILING MERCURY & URANUS TALK		*Lyn*
PLANET	SIGN	HOUSE
MERCURY	*Virgo*	*3rd*
Thinking	*To Improve*	*Thinking*
URANUS	*Gemini*	*11th*
Revolutionizing	*Thinking*	*(is my) Goal*

Comment on the Combination, that is, how you see these two Keyphrases side by side:

They appear to be on the same team, sort of. The idea springs to mind that where 'improving' fails in its purpose 'revolution' will take over. Something will rise up, one way or the other, to upgrade (Uranus Cloud Keyword) my thinking. In fact, this has occurred a number of times in my life, in small or large ways, some smooth and some rough.

Listen to what Uranus is Saying to Mercury:

*'Carry on thinking to improve thinking but be prepared and open to radically change your actual attitude to thinking itself - or rather, **have** it changed. This is not something you will be able to think about much, or predict. Think about that, that the change will come one way or the other, as it will - in a flash maybe. Don't wait up. Be loose. Be free of expectations. My upgrades will come out of the blue!'*

cont'd

***Example* PROFILING MERCURY & URANUS TALK *Lyn*-cont'd**

Have Mercury ask a question of Uranus and 'listen' for Uranus's response. Bear in mind that if its response does not come straightaway, it will come later when you are not expecting it - as ever, out of the blue - and not necessarily in the way or form that you expected either.

"How can I stop or limit you 'overloading' my mind as if you were some cosmic website downloading masses of data to my little computer brain?"

Answer: *Clear out unwanted thoughts and ideas.*

(Optional) Continue the dialogue or questions and answers as long as you like (on extra paper). But actually it will be for as long as, and when, Uranus likes.

☿♅ *PROFILING MERCURY & URANUS TALK:*

PLANET	SIGN	HOUSE
MERCURY		
URANUS		

Comment on the Combination, that is, how you see these two
Keyphrases side by side:

Listen to what Uranus is Saying to Mercury:

cont'd

☿♅ *PROFILING MERCURY & URANUS TALK:* cont'd

Have Mercury ask a question of Uranus and 'listen' for Uranus's response. Bear in mind that if its response does not come straightaway, it will come later when you are not expecting it - as ever, out of the blue - and not necessarily in the way or form that you expected either.

(Optional) Continue the dialogue or questions and answers as long as you like (in space provided or on separate paper). But actually it will be for as long as, and when, Uranus likes.

Venus & Neptune

The Lovers

We now enter the Realm of the Heart. Following upon *The Lights* and *The Links*, we now encounter *The Lovers*.

I call them *The Lovers* as they are essentially both about the expression and experience of that which makes life worth living in an emotional, sensual, artistic and/or spiritual way.

In the context of the planetary pairs or *octaves* that are the subject of Exercises 4 to 12, Venus, as the lower octave here, is a *personal sense of love*, expressed as *affection, beauty, value, attractiveness, pleasure, art, etc.* while Neptune is its higher octave, that is, *a universal sense of love*, or *compassion, inspiration, peace and upliftment born of a sensitivity and attunement to higher or finer dimensions*.

So, Venus shows how we may give form to whatever makes life *agreeable, enjoyable or satisfying*, while Neptune is calling us all from a metaphysical level towards something of transcendental meaning that goes beyond personal satisfaction into the *transformative realms of healing, imagination (channelling) and at-one-ment*.

As pointed out earlier, it will be found that the Profiling of this, and the other planetary pairs, is rather like tuning an instrument. The lower octave resonates with the higher octave thereby properly attuning you to these planetary energies.

In the case of Neptune and Venus, one product of this attunement could be the creation of a more romantic sense of life which sees something or someone, or everything and everyone, as sacred and as living out some meaningful role in some great myth. However, because this 'romance' is so enchanting and longed for, such attunement can be illusory and eventually disappointing. A case of true romance or fanciful romance.

And yet 'all roads lead to Rome', for suffering romantic

illusions is all on the way to finding the real thing: *selfless love*, which is the essence of Neptune. One could say that suffering is the way *to* love, but not the way *of* love. We have to *fall* in love in order to eventually *ascend* to a higher expression of love. And note here how the meanings of Venus and Neptune can intertwine, *Lovers* that they are!

With Venus and Neptune we also need to consider more the issue of *worth*. Venus is worth translated into *attractive, pleasurable or valuable objects*, one of which includes *money*, that great and terrible symbol of worth itself. Venus is also *self-worth or talent*.

Neptune is worth of an *intangible* kind, such as *imagination*; a worth that is priceless and free all at the same time. This could all be summed up as with the song title *Can't Buy Me Love*, the ultimate realization and denouement of the Venus/Neptune story – *Love and Peace*, no less.

So with Profiling Venus and Neptune, this is like one scale of values or description of love harmonizing, or not, with another scale and description. Again though, be aware that there can be cross-talk between any planetary pair, for example the Moon and Mars, something which we will explore in *Dynamic Interactive Astrology – Level Two – The Aspects*.

So you may now begin Profiling VENUS and then proceed when ready to Profiling NEPTUNE as you did with Mercury and Uranus previously and with the Sun and Moon before that.

The Lovers being what they are, you may find it advantageous to Profile both before you offer up just the one of them. This is because you may find how the Profiling of the one affects your Profiling of the other. This means that you may find that you need to edit what you have done for Venus after inner promptings felt through doing Neptune – and vice versa.

REMINDER! SCAN OR PHOTOCOPY THE EXERCISES so you can use them more than once. Use *extra paper if required* in order to complete the Exercises to your satisfaction.

Exercise 7 - Profiling Venus

The questions or assignments are initially what you yourself answer and perform, and subsequently what you can apply to others.

1. In the table below headed ♀ *PROFILING VENUS,* **after** the *Example,* insert the position of VENUS by SIGN and HOUSE (as given in your chart) in the third row in the relevant columns. *Enter name top-right.*

2. From the **Primary Dynamic Keywords** on page 251 freely select **one** keyword each for VENUS, SIGN and HOUSE and then insert them in the fourth row in the appropriate columns as in the *Example* below. You now have your Venus Keyphrase on the fourth row, which for our Example of Marilyn Monroe can read: "(With my) Beauty and Art (I) Lead (my) Culture."

Example		*Marilyn Monroe*
PLANET	SIGN	HOUSE
VENUS	*Aries*	*9th*
Beauty/Art	*To Lead*	*Culture*

Important Note: Because Venus is closer to the Sun than the Earth is, it is never more than two Signs away *from* the Sun. This means that it is often placed in the same Sign and/or House as the Sun. If this is the case, you may find it useful to separate out the Living (Sun) from the Socio-Sensual (Venus) by choosing keywords for the Sign and House of Venus that are significantly different from your Sun's Sign and House keywords.

Gender Note: As Venus is essentially a Planet of the *feminine,* whereas it usually directly describes certain feminine qualities and traits for a female individual, for a male such qualities can describe his *anima* (inner feminine) and so are often seen or looked for in a female, but by no means always.

♀ *PROFILING VENUS:*		
PLANET	SIGN	HOUSE
VENUS		

3. When you have done the above, answer the following questions. While doing so you may refer to the appropriate Keyword Clouds – which are found in the Toolkit on page 261 – if you feel the need to jog your mind, enhance meaning or stimulate your imagination.

Keyword Clouds also broaden your knowledge of astrological symbolism and correspondences generally.

Venus Questions

☺ *If you cannot answer any question come back to it later.*

a) Record or write down freely the feelings, thoughts and impressions that you experience on reading and pondering your Venus Keyphrase.

b) What character traits would you say were evidence or expressions of your Venus Keyphrase?

c) What events, situations or feelings, if any, would you say are a testament to your being true to your Venus Keyphrase?

d) What events, feelings or situations, if any, would you say are a testament to your NOT being true to your Venus Keyphrase? How could you move on through or out of such situations in order to embody or realize your Venus Keyphrase?

e) In what ways does your Venus Keyphrase show how you attract others or win them over? Or lose out with others or run into relationship difficulties?

f) What does your Venus Keyphrase tell you about your natural talents? Are you appreciating them? Are you making the most of them?

g) In what ways does being true to your Venus Keyphrase bring happiness, value and beauty into your life, and the lives of others? How or why are you possibly NOT being true to it and how does that inhibit happiness, value and beauty coming into your life and the lives of those around you?

h) How do you feel the nature of your Venus Keyphrase or Profile affects the quality of life, particularly with regard to the House position keyword?

i) How do you feel or think the expression and qualities of your Venus Keyphrase affected the initial development of your love and social relationships? Comment on this.

j) To what degree and in what way has your Venus Keyphrase contributed, or NOT, to your financial situation or earning power?

k) Make a summing up statement concerning all of the above. Doing this will reveal to you how through using *Dynamic Interactive Astrology* you are becoming not only versed in astrology, but becoming more aware of yourself as a unique individual. Feel free to share parts of your Summary Statement in the *Dynamic Interactive Astrology Facebook Group* at: www.facebook.com/groups/dynamicinteractiveastrology

Additional Venus Exercises

It is recommended that having completed the above, you do it all again, now or later, choosing another set of Dynamic Keywords to make a different Venus, Sign and House Keyphrase.

This gives you another slant on the chart/person's dynamics and characteristics.

You can repeat this with alternative keywords as many times as you like or see fit. You can also refer to the relevant Keyword Clouds for extra, sometimes more intermediate or advanced keywords.

Exercise 8 - Profiling Neptune

The questions or assignments are initially what you yourself answer and perform, and subsequently what you can apply to others.

1. In the table below headed ♆ *PROFILING NEPTUNE*, following the *Example*, insert the position of NEPTUNE by SIGN and HOUSE (as given in your chart) in the third row in the relevant columns. *Enter name top-right.*

2. From the **Primary Dynamic Keywords** on page 251 freely select **one** keyword each for NEPTUNE, SIGN and HOUSE and then insert them in the fourth row in the appropriate columns as in the *Example* below. You now have your Neptune Keyphrase on the fourth row, which for our Example of Keith Richards could be: "(My) Public Image (is one that is) Inspiring (and is Inspired by) Harmonizing (with my band and my fans)."

Example		*Keith Richards*
PLANET	SIGN	HOUSE
NEPTUNE	*Libra*	*10th*
Inspiring	*To Harmonize*	*(type of) Public Image*

Important Note 1 – As Neptune is one of the three slow-moving Outer Planets (along with Uranus and Pluto), the energies or qualities of its Sign position apply to a whole 13-14 year-long generation, the time it takes for it to transit one Sign.

This means that the Neptunian energy of Attuning, Inspiring and Sensitizing applies itself to matters regarding that Sign. So in our *Example*, Keith Richards was part of a whole Neptune in Libra generation that was "Inspiring to Harmonize" – or whatever Keyphrase you choose for this Planet/Sign position –

particularly when they came of age. Consider how, especially in the light of his Neptune House position, he was an icon of the 1960s' Flower Power/Peace and Love (Libra) generation!

Important Note 2 – In the context of its Sign and/or House position, bear in mind that Neptune is always about having some dream or ideal to better the/your world – or about finding the means to escape *from* the world.

It can be useful to reverse the Planet and Sign keywords, while shifting the tense. So in our *Example* it could read "Harmonizing to Inspire" (type of) Public Image.

But it is the *House* position that indicates how this generational effect applies to you as an individual, or how you as an individual apply yourself to it. The personal effect of Neptune is revealed in more detail by any Aspects to it, the stuff of *Dynamic Interactive Astrology – Level Two*.

You can also omit the Sign keyword altogether, in our *Example* giving simply "Inspiring Public Image" or using Cloud Keywords: "Drugging or Addicting Public Image". Or just "Music Profession".

Generally speaking, always let your imagination loose with the keywords – especially with Neptune as it is the Planet of Imagination. *Let the Keywords Flow.*

♆ *PROFILING NEPTUNE:*		
PLANET	SIGN	HOUSE
NEPTUNE		

3. When you have done the above to your satisfaction, answer the following Questions, referring to the appropriate Keyword Clouds if you feel the need to jog your mind, enhance meaning or stimulate your imagination.

Keyword Clouds also broaden your knowledge of astrological symbolism and correspondences generally.

Neptune Questions
☺ *If you cannot answer any question come back to it later.*

a) Record or write down freely the feelings, thoughts and impressions that you experience on reading and pondering your Neptune Keyphrase.

b) What character traits would you say were evidence or expressions of your Neptune Keyphrase?

c) What events, situations or feelings, if any, would you say are a testament to your being true to your Neptune Keyphrase?

d) What events, feelings or situations, if any, would you say are a testament to your NOT being true to your Neptune Keyphrase? How could you move on through or out of such situations in order to embody or realize your Neptune Keyphrase?

e) In the context of your Neptune Keyphrase, what would you say your personal dream or idealistic goal is? What do you do, or can you do, to make this dream a reality?

f) As Neptune is such a spiritual influence, as opposed to an egotistical or materialistic one, in what ways is it possible that being true to your Neptune Keyphrase has been compromised, inhibited or confused by giving too much consideration to physical, material or financial issues, or to gratifying your ego? To follow your dream you may very well need to get by with less materially, or not be recognized (initially, at least), which means not conforming to the conventions of the ego/material world and its demanding/limiting ways.

g) As sensitivity is such a predominant quality of Neptune, in what ways, if any, has sensitivity affected and figured in your life? If you have not used the 'Sensitizing' keyword in your Keyphrase it could be helpful to do so for answering this question. Also, consider how sensitivity has been an asset (e.g. healing, creativity), and/or where it has become a liability (e.g. victimhood, poor health).

h) In what way, if any, have addictions, seductive influences or evasion strategies prevented you from following your dream, or sabotaged it, as described by your Neptune Keyphrase? Are any of these Neptunian temptations still doing this in any way? In what way could your Neptune Keyphrase help you to turn around (make positive) any such temptations or weaknesses? What might this say about any propensity toward victimhood, which is effectively born of oversensitivity or unexpressed sensitivity?

i) In what ways, if any, do you look for your dream or ideal in another person, an animal, or some material object? Consider your answer to this very honestly, and how it is possibly reflected in your Neptune Keyphrase(s). If the answer is in the affirmative in any way, then reflect on this and then comment.

j) Do you feel the expression and qualities of your Neptune Keyphrase arose spontaneously to you early on in life, in your childhood? If so, in what way? And was there a time when they ceased to do so, partially or completely? If so, how or why did this happen? And how could you rekindle them?

k) Have a look at all the keywords in the Neptune Cloud on page 266 and consider the ones you identify with in any way, and what positive or negative feelings or memories they prompt. Then set about ACCEPTING all of those feelings and experiences as all part of Neptune's plan for you. For where Neptune is concerned there is no 'right' or 'wrong' as we generally understand these terms. Wherever the river of your life flows, that is where it is supposed to flow. It is in being more consciously accepting of the flow that the course of your river becomes truer to itself.

l) Make a summing up statement concerning all of the above. Doing this will reveal to you how through using *Dynamic Interactive Astrology* you are becoming not only versed in astrology, but becoming more aware of yourself as a unique individual. Feel free to share parts of your Summary Statement in the *Dynamic Interactive Astrology Facebook Group* at: www. facebook.com/groups/dynamicinteractiveastrology

Additional Neptune Exercises

It is recommended that having completed the above, you do it all again, now or later, choosing another set of Dynamic Keywords to make a different Neptune, Sign and House Keyphrase.

This gives you another slant on the chart/person's dynamics and characteristics.

You can repeat this with alternative keywords as many times as you like or see fit. You can also refer to the relevant Keyword Clouds for extra, sometimes more intermediate or advanced keywords.

Exercise 9 - Profiling Venus & Neptune Marriage

This is an exercise that serves to heighten your sense of what these two Planets mean to you, and how they feel to you. This enables you to resonate with Venus and Neptune in your own and others' birth charts. This means that you begin to appreciate more how *love* and *worth* figure in your life, and the lives of others – on both tangible (Venus) and intangible (Neptune) levels.

Venus and Neptune are both social/emotional Planets. So here is how to get in touch with them with respect to how you relate to both inner and outer, spiritual and physical, worlds.

1. Initially 'prime' your mind by having a good look at both the Venus and the Neptune Clouds on pages 261 and 266. This will make you more *resonant* with their meaning and facilitate their 'marriage'.

2. In the table below headed ♀ ♆ *PROFILING VENUS & NEPTUNE MARRIAGE*, following the *Example*, insert the position of VENUS by SIGN and HOUSE (as given in your chart) in the third row in the relevant columns. *Enter name top-right.* See *Example* below.

3. From the **Primary Dynamic Keywords** on page 251 freely select **one** keyword each for VENUS, SIGN and HOUSE and then insert them in the fourth row in the appropriate columns as in the *Example* below. Note: Again, if you wish, you may use the same keywords as you used before in Exercise 7. Or you may use keywords found in the Venus Cloud on page 261.

4. Now, in the same table below headed ♀ ♆ *PROFILING VENUS & NEPTUNE MARRIAGE*, following the *Example*, insert the position of NEPTUNE by SIGN and HOUSE (as given in your chart) in the fifth row in the relevant columns.

5. From the **Primary Dynamic Keywords**, freely select **one** keyword each for NEPTUNE, SIGN and HOUSE and then insert them in the sixth row in the appropriate columns as in the *Example* below. Note: Again, if you wish, you may use the same keywords as you used before in Exercise 8. Or you may use

keywords found in the Neptune Cloud on page 266.

6. Now respond to the questions that follow in the next rows of the table (starting with Comment on the Combination, that is, how you see these two Keyphrases side by side). See *Example* following.

Example PROFILING VENUS & NEPTUNE MARRIAGE *Lyn*		
PLANET	SIGN	HOUSE
VENUS	*Libra*	*3rd*
Art	*To Beautify*	*(with) Words*
NEPTUNE	*Libra*	*3rd*
Meditating	*To Harmonize*	*(with) Everyday Life*

Comment on how you see these two Keyphrases side by side, on how they combine:

Having both Planets in the same Sign and House naturally helps the Marriage - like they're both on the same hymn sheet! And this makes me aware that not everyone has the same Venus and Neptune positions as me (that is, both in the same Sign and House), and that they find it harder or easier to 'marry' these two Lovers. I do have a keen sense of beauty and harmony on an everyday level. I feel a natural inclination to be pleasant and friendly with strangers I meet. I am looking to be 'in love' daily, which paradoxically make me quite demanding of myself and others - and one other in particular, my wife! But the more Neptunian I am - the more I meditate to harmonize - the less I am demanding of others, and them of me, as a climate of acceptance is created. All this can be quite subtle and complex as demonstrated a few days before the time of writing this. I encountered a neighbor (3rd House) who I only speak with very occasionally, but I could tell he was reaching out to me for

cont'd

Example *PROFILING VENUS & NEPTUNE MARRIAGE Lyn* **cont'd**

something. It was slightly awkward at first before I managed to combine a purely social chit-chat (Venus) with something more finely tuned (Neptune). So I talked with him longer than usual and the conversation became quite spiritual and touched on sensitive areas. Yet at the same time I felt aware that I could not extend myself to him that much socially. But yet again, I am still pondering on how I could harmonize more with him as I still feel he is yearning for something - a more spiritual connection maybe, or just company for someone who I sensed was quite withdrawn inside of himself. So, an ongoing Venus and Neptune in Libra in the 3rd House story!

Now look at your Neptune Keyphrase and imagine a message of love and worth (from a song, literature, of your own making, or from wherever you like) that you'd like to send to your Venus, the part of you that is looking to give and receive love.

"Love is all around"

Now look at your Venus Keyphrase again and then make an offering or pledge of love and worth to Neptune on high, like a deposit in the cosmic/heavenly bank.

Art to Beautify with Words...I shall make a point of putting out some form of invitation to talk further with my neighbor at the next opportunity to connect more with what he is yearning for, and possibly what I am looking for too.

This sends a receipt in the form of the love and worth message Neptune has just made, that is, what is expressed in your Neptune Keyphrase (enter this).

Meditating to Harmonize (with) Everyday Life

Comment:

There is so much unrecognized beauty in the world!

♀♆ *PROFILING VENUS & NEPTUNE MARRIAGE:*

PLANET	SIGN	HOUSE
VENUS		
NEPTUNE		

Comment on how you see these two Keyphrases side by side, on how they combine:

cont'd

♀♆ *PROFILING VENUS & NEPTUNE MARRIAGE:*
cont'd

Look at your Neptune Keyphrase and imagine a message of love and worth (from a song, literature, of your own making, or from wherever you like) that you'd like to send to your Venus, the part of you that is looking to give and receive love:

Now look at your Venus Keyphrase again and then make an offering or pledge of love and worth to Neptune on high, like a deposit in the cosmic/heavenly bank.

This sends a receipt in the form of the love and worth message Neptune has just made, that is, what is expressed in your Neptune Keyphrase. Comment:

Additional Venus & Neptune Marriage Exercises

You can now, if you wish it or feel it, make a new Neptune Keyphrase and start a new cycle of giving and receiving love and worth all over again – and as many times as you like – creating a new Venus Keyphrase too if you wish it or feel it.

This is Neptune and Venus *literally* making Love.

Mars & Pluto

The Forces

We now enter the Realm of Actualization, the 'make it happen' zone. Following upon *The Lights, The Links and The Lovers*, now we encounter *The Forces*.

As you know, in Exercises 4 to 12 we are concerned with Profiling three planetary pairs each of which are made up of a lower and a higher octave. In all cases the lower octave is an *inner or personal* planet which represents a power you have some control over, while the higher octave is an *outer or transpersonal planet* which we have no control over, other than the way in which a personal planet relates to it and expresses it.

In this regard, I call the planetary pair that is Mars and Pluto *The Forces* as they are essentially both about the expression and experience of that which makes things happen or actively mobilizes people and things.

Mars, the lower octave, is a *personal sense of force*, expressed as *drive, desire, self-assertion, the urge to act or get, etc.* while Pluto is its higher octave, that is, *an urge born of some deeper or collective desire, divine will, an overriding influence, the power of fate itself.*

At a basic level it could be said that Mars symbolizes that part of us that is out for itself, *pursuing* its own gratification and survival needs. How it goes about this and how successful it is in this *quest* can make an enormous difference to how *effective* one feels, which in turn influences many other, if not all, parts of one's personality and life. Naturally, such *'selfishness'* is qualified by who or what one is questing for, as Mars can be the *champion* or *hunter* who protects and provides for those in one's 'tribe' – that is, whoever or whatever is of concern to one.

This basic, primal or even primitive quality of Mars is seen in Pluto, but at a far *deeper, darker* and *primordial* level. It goes beyond one's personal desires and somehow hooks up with something that was there on the first day – reflecting *birth* – and will be there on the last day – *death*. Pluto is also *rebirth and transformation*. Physiologically Pluto governs the older parts of the brain, the *reptilian brain* and *limbic system*. Here lie *powers and compulsions* born of *ancient fears and urges*.

Both Mars and Pluto are very influential regarding *sexuality* in the sense of *'going for it'* or *'pulling it'*, something which is usually, but certainly not exclusively, the concern of male sexuality. The difference between these two Forces is well demonstrated here if one sees 'planting the seed' as up to Mars, while impregnation is down to Pluto – fate, in fact. There is of course a 'chicken and egg' issue here, in that Mars has to be attracted by someone or something – the province of Venus; while Pluto is subject to the realm of mystery, Neptune.

In arranging these six planets as three planetary pairs it will be found that the Profiling of each pair is rather like tuning an instrument. The lower octave resonates with the higher octave thereby properly attuning you to those planetary energies.

In the case of Pluto and Mars, one product of this attunement could be the creation of a stronger or more defined sense of one's *physical effectiveness* (Mars) and *psychological influence* (Pluto), and thereby the connection between deep, possibly *hidden*, feelings (Pluto) and the *assertion* or expression of those feelings (Mars). In other words, the emphasizing of the one can automatically empower the other, and vice versa. This is important because there can be a strong disinclination to either dare to say and do what you want (Mars) or delve down into one's deeper emotions and discover the power that dwells therein (Pluto). The reason for this disinclination is often down to being thwarted or defeated (Mars) or disempowered or abused (Pluto) at some earlier stage of life.

All of this could be said to be down to the astrological fact that Mars and Pluto – along with Saturn – are described as the *Malefics*. This denotes these Planets as having more potential to produce negative emotions and states than the other Planets can. Consequently these Planets' qualities are more likely to be pushed down into the unconscious where they take the form of one's Shadow. Negatively expressed, Mars can be *stress, anger, violence, war, etc.*; Pluto can be *evil, horror, hell, rape, etc.*

Because of this Malefic quality, Profiling Mars and Pluto can be quite difficult, but commensurately rewarding when given a positive expression such as *energizing or promoting* (Mars) something good, or *empowering or influencing* (Pluto) in a healthy way. Experiencing these Planets can be felt as one kind of Force contacting or rubbing up against another kind of Force. This can be very telling (and possibly not comfortable) with regard to how effectively (or not) one handles the exterior and interior worlds that life presents us with. Profiling these two Planets can amount to the question: "Are you a force to be reckoned with, or at the mercy of some other force – or happy to be an 'also ran' or not in any race at all?"

For all the above reasons, the Profiling of Mars and Pluto (and Saturn in Exercise 14) is designed to be more extensive and exhaustive than the Profiling of other Planets.

So you may now begin Profiling MARS and then proceed when ready to Profiling PLUTO as you did with the other planetary pairs before this.

As with *The Lovers*, you may find it advantageous to Profile both before you complete or offer up just the one of them. This is because you may find how the Profiling of the one affects your Profiling of the other. This means that you may find that you need to edit what you have done for Mars after deeper promptings felt through doing Pluto – and vice versa.

Exercise 10 - Profiling Mars

The questions or assignments are initially what you yourself answer and perform, and subsequently what you can apply to others.

1. In the table below headed ♂ *PROFILING MARS*, following the *Example*, insert the position of MARS by SIGN and HOUSE (as given in your chart) in the third row in the relevant columns. *Enter name top-right.*

2. From the **Primary Dynamic Keywords** on page 251 freely select **one** keyword each for MARS, SIGN and HOUSE and then insert them in the fourth row in the appropriate columns as in the *Example* below. You now have your Mars Keyphrase on the fourth row, which for our Example of Muhammad Ali asserts: "(My) Drive Substantiates (my own and others') Beliefs."

Example		*Muhammad Ali*
PLANET	SIGN	HOUSE
MARS	*Taurus*	*9th*
Drive	*To Substantiate*	*Beliefs*

Important Note: Mars is the first Planet outside the orbit of the Earth, pointing away from the Sun into darkness and the unknown, a suitable position for the Planet of Courage and Pioneering. This position also means that it can – unlike Venus and Mercury which are within Earth's orbit – be placed in any Sign of the Zodiac, reflecting its independent quality.

Gender Note: As Mars is essentially a Planet of the *masculine*, whereas it usually directly describes certain masculine qualities and traits for a male individual, for a female such qualities can describe her *animus* (inner masculine) and so are often seen or looked for in a male, but by no means always.

Example Note: Ali's religious beliefs – as a Muslim and eventually as a Sufi – moved him to resist the draft into the military at the time of the Vietnam War, which in turn gave rise to him losing his boxing license. He stuck to his guns and eventually the Supreme Court overturned the conviction. One could also say that as a boxer, the 'greatest', he also *substantiated* his fans' *belief* in him.

♂ *PROFILING MARS:*		
PLANET	SIGN	HOUSE
MARS		

3. When you have done the above to your satisfaction, answer the following Questions referring to the appropriate Keyword Clouds if you feel the need to jog your mind, enhance meaning or stimulate your imagination.

Keyword Clouds also broaden your knowledge of astrological symbolism and correspondences generally.

Mars Questions

☺ *If you cannot answer any question come back to it later.*

a) Record or write down freely the feelings, thoughts and impressions that you experience on reading and pondering your Mars Keyphrase.

b) What character traits would you say were evidence or expressions of your Mars Keyphrase?

c) What events, situations or feelings, if any, would you say are a testament to your being true to your Mars Keyphrase?

d) What events, feelings or situations, if any, would you say are a testament to your NOT being true to your Mars Keyphrase? How could you move on through or out of such situations in order to embody or realize your Mars Keyphrase?

e) In the context of your Mars Keyphrase, what, if anything, makes you angry? By the same token, how might this lead you to have violent feelings, or a fear of violence?

f) In the light of your answer to question (e) what can you do to transmute such anger into positive action – using your Keyphrase as a guide or clue to this, adjusting the keywords in it if necessary?

g) With your Mars Keyphrase in mind, do you have a 'quest' in life – something for which you would fight, suffer hardship or go the extra mile?

h) Imagine Mars as a sword – *your* sword. Now imagine what you are doing with your sword. Are you wielding it to assert or defend what is important to you? Or are you leaving it somewhere for someone else to pick up? Or, if you are holding it, is it turned inwards or outwards? Reflect honestly on your findings and feelings here – again using your Keyphrase as a prompt or guide. Explore and comment.

i) Mars can be regarded as your 'edge' – a hard aspect of your personality, something that can often be relegated to your Shadow, that is, seen as not 'nice' or antisocial, or dangerous, and then projected on to others or the world at large. In the light of the above questions and answers, what is the nature and status of your 'edge'? To facilitate this, try using the keyword 'Effectiveness' for Mars in your Keyphrase.

j) Mars energy is most easily expressed straightforwardly, directly and honestly. How does your Keyphrase facilitate, or not, being straightforward, direct and honest? If you feel it compromises you, how could you move through or round this compromising of your intent?

k) In a similar way to the previous question, Mars energy is about decisiveness. So again, how does your Keyphrase facilitate, or not, being decisive? If you feel it compromises you in this respect, making you feel indecisive and undecided, how could you move through or round this compromising of your decision-making ability? Try different keywords and Keyphrases to assist you here.

l) If you are male, what does your Mars Keyphrase say about what kind of man you are, and about your sex drive? If you are female, what does your Mars Keyphrase say about the kind of man you attract or attracted to, or about your *animus* or inner masculine, and about your sex drive?

m) Mars is all about *raw energy* for the use of. How much energy you have or do not have can be more often than not directly related to how well you are expressing your Mars, as described by your Mars Keyphrase or Keyphrases. In what ways is the expression of your Mars qualities, as here revealed, releasing or repressing your energy supply?

n) Make a summing up statement concerning all of the above. Doing this will reveal to you how through using *Dynamic Interactive Astrology* you are becoming not only versed in astrology, but becoming more aware of yourself as a unique individual. Feel free to share parts of your Summary Statement in the *Dynamic Interactive Astrology Facebook Group* at: www.facebook.com/groups/dynamicinteractiveastrology

Additional Mars Exercises

It is recommended that having completed the above, you do it all again, now or later, choosing another set of Dynamic Keywords to make a different Mars, Sign and House Keyphrase.

This gives you another slant on the chart/person's dynamics and characteristics.

You can repeat this with alternative keywords as many times as you like or see fit. You can also refer to the relevant Keyword Clouds for extra, sometimes more intermediate or advanced keywords.

Exercise 11 - Profiling Pluto

The questions or assignments are initially what you yourself answer and perform, and subsequently what you can apply to others.

1. In the table below headed ♇ *PROFILING PLUTO*, following the *Example*, insert the position of PLUTO by SIGN and HOUSE (as given in your chart) in the third row in the relevant columns. *Enter name top-right.*

2. From the **Primary Dynamic Keywords** on page 251 freely select **one** keyword each for PLUTO, SIGN and HOUSE and then insert them in the fourth row in the appropriate columns as in the *Example* below. You now have your Pluto Keyphrase on the fourth row, which for our Example of Princess Diana could state: "(I have the) Power to Serve (through) Intimacy (that is, by bringing people closer together)."

Example		*Princess Diana*
PLANET	SIGN	HOUSE
PLUTO	*Virgo*	*8th*
Empowering	*To Serve*	*(through) Intimacy*

Important Note 1 – As Pluto is one of the three slow-moving Outer Planets, the energies or qualities of its Sign position apply to a whole 15-20 year-long generation, the time it takes for it to transit one Sign. This means that the Plutonian energy of Empowering, Intensifying and Transforming applies itself to matters regarding that Sign which it is in. So in our *Example*, Diana was part of a whole Pluto in Virgo generation that was "Empowering to Serve" – or whatever Keyphrase you choose for this Planet/Sign position – particularly when they come of age. As the 'People's Princess' Diana was very much using her power of position to serve the interests of the common people.

Important Note 2 – In the context of its Sign and/or House position, bear in mind that Pluto is always about gaining some *deeper* and more *profound* sense of what life is about. This 'gain' may come through some kind of *crisis*, as this is one way Pluto has of *eliminating* anything less than *authentic*. "No gain without pain" could be a Plutonian slogan.

It helps to Profile Pluto by allowing the keywords to resonate at as deep a level as possible, focusing perhaps on your root chakra (at your perineum) as you do so. *Let the Keywords Penetrate.*

It can also be useful to reverse the Planet and Sign keywords, while shifting the tense. So in our *Example* it could read, "Serving to Empower (through) Intimacy."

But it is the *House* position that indicates how this generational effect applies to you as an individual, or how you as an individual apply yourself to it. The personal effect of Pluto is revealed in more detail by any Aspects to it, the stuff of *Dynamic Interactive Astrology – Level Two.*

You can also omit the Sign keyword altogether, in our *Example* giving just "Empowering through Intimacy." But the profundity of Princess Diana's life could simply be seen by changing the 8th House keyword along with the tense of the Pluto keyword: "Empowered by Death."

♇ *PROFILING PLUTO:*		
PLANET	SIGN	HOUSE
PLUTO		

3. When you have done the above to your satisfaction, answer the following Questions, referring to the appropriate Keyword Clouds if you feel the need to jog your mind, enhance meaning or stimulate your imagination.

Keyword Clouds, beginning on page 257, also broaden your knowledge of astrological symbolism and correspondences generally.

Pluto Questions

☺ *If you cannot answer any question come back to it later.*

a) Record or write down freely the feelings, thoughts and impressions that you experience on reading and pondering your Pluto Keyphrase.

b) What character traits would you say were evidence or expressions of your Pluto Keyphrase?

c) What events, situations or feelings, if any, would you say are a testament to your being true to your Pluto Keyphrase?

d) What events, feelings or situations, if any, would you say are a testament to your NOT being true to your Pluto Keyphrase? How could you move on through or out of such situations in order to embody or realize your Pluto Keyphrase?

e) Considering your Pluto Keyphrase, what would you say is the dimension of your personality and life that has undergone the most transformation (so far)? Hint: try using 'Transforming' as the Pluto keyword in your Keyphrase, if you haven't already.

f) In what way, if any, has such transformation empowered or disempowered yourself or others? If 'disempowered', in what way could you transform *that*, using the keywords as clues if necessary?

g) What does your Pluto Keyphrase tell you about any crises in your life? What does it tell you about how you handle a crisis, and how this is reflected in your Keyphrase? Transform your Keyphrase itself if necessary in order to accomplish this.

h) Using 'Death' as your Pluto keyword in your Pluto Keyphrase, and changing the Sign and House keywords if you see fit, what does this tell you about your feelings or attitude concerning death?

i) As far as Pluto is concerned, 'Transformation is the name of game.' So have you in any way felt how some or all of the above exercises have purged and transformed you, or are possibly about to do so?

j) As Pluto is one of the 'Shadow' Planets *this is a particularly difficult exercise and so is optional!*

Have a look at the keywords in the Pluto Cloud and consider just one you identify with in a way that reminds you personally of an event that involved the darker side of life. Next consider how this keyword possibly has something to do with your Shadow in the sense of it being associated with whatever you have been led to believe is socially unacceptable or unattractive.

Now using this Pluto keyword, create a new Pluto Keyphrase that could bring your Shadow to light by drawing to the surface something powerful that has hitherto been repressed by not owning this power.

Example (Lyn): I picked the keyword 'Ruthlessness', something which reminded me of how I dealt with a life and death situation involving two people very close to me. 'Ruthlessness' appears to be cold and cruel, so something I naturally try to avoid – but this would indicate something about/in my Shadow.

Now I create the Keyphrase "Ruthlessness to Rule (Leo) over Self (1st House)." If I had let myself become emotionally overwhelmed I would have ill-served both people. To others I may have seemed to be on auto-pilot and therefore possibly cold and unfeeling, but this is how I was able to successfully manage the situation. This put me permanently in touch with an element of my personality that has empowered me in many ways, not least of all conferring on me a sound sense of priorities. Another thing it taught me was that sometimes it doesn't matter if others don't know how I am feeling – as long as I myself know how I am feeling – and in the above instance I was going through hell!

j) As Pluto is one of the 'Shadow' Planets (Continued)

k) Make a summing up statement concerning all of the above. Doing this will reveal to you how through using *Dynamic Interactive Astrology* you are becoming not only versed in astrology, but becoming more aware of yourself as a unique individual. Feel free to share parts of your Summary Statement in the *Dynamic Interactive Astrology Facebook Group* at: www.facebook.com/groups/dynamicinteractiveastrology

Additional Pluto Exercises

It is recommended that having completed the above, you do it all again, now or later, choosing another set of Dynamic Keywords to make a different Pluto, Sign and House Keyphrase.

This gives you another slant on the chart/person's dynamics and characteristics.

You can repeat this with alternative keywords as many times as you like or see fit. You can also refer to the relevant Keyword Clouds on page 257 for extra, sometimes more advanced, keywords.

Exercise 12 - Profiling Mars & Pluto Alliance

This is an exercise that serves to heighten your sense of what these two Planets mean to you, and how they feel to you. This enables you to resonate with Mars and Pluto in your own and others' birth charts. This means that you begin to appreciate more how *drive* and *power* figure in your life, and the lives of others – on both individual (Mars) and collective (Pluto) levels.

Mars and Pluto are go-getter/survival Planets and so we need to get in touch with them with respect to how effective we can be in individual and collective, physical and spiritual, spheres.

1. Initially 'prime' your mind by having a good look at both the Mars and the Pluto Clouds on pages 262 and 267. This will make you more *resonant* with their meaning and facilitate their 'alliance'.

2. In the table below headed ♂♇ *PROFILING MARS & PLUTO ALLIANCE*, following the *Example*, insert the position of MARS by SIGN and HOUSE (as given in your chart) in the third row in the relevant columns. *Enter name top-right.* See *Example* below.

3. From the **Primary Dynamic Keywords**, freely select **one** keyword each for MARS, SIGN and HOUSE and then insert them in the appropriate columns as in the *Example* below. Note: Again, if you wish, you may use the same keywords as you used before in Exercise 10. Or you may use keywords found in the Mars Cloud on page 262.

4. Now, in the same table below headed ♂♇ *PROFILING MARS & PLUTO ALLIANCE*, following the *Example*, insert the position of PLUTO by SIGN and HOUSE (as given in your chart) in the fifth row in the relevant columns.

5. From the **Primary Dynamic Keywords** on page 251 freely select **one** keyword each for PLUTO, SIGN and HOUSE and then insert them in the sixth row in the appropriate columns as in the *Example* below. Note: Again, if you wish, you may use the same keywords as you used before in Exercise 11. Or you may

use keywords found in the Pluto Cloud on page 267.

6. Now respond to the questions that follow in the next rows of the table (starting with 'Comment on the Combination', that is, how you see these two Keyphrases side by side:). See *Example* below.

PLANET	SIGN	HOUSE
***Example* PROFILING MARS & PLUTO ALLIANCE**		***Lyn***
MARS	*Libra*	*3rd*
Drive	*To Reconcile*	*(with) Words*
PLUTO	*Leo*	*1st*
Empowering	*To Dramatize*	*Self*

Comment on how you see these two Keyphrases side by side, on how they combine:

This cannot help but remind me of how I work as an astrological consultant. My aim or quest is to bring resolution and harmony to the situation of my client, and I dramatize both my own influence and the personality of my client in order that 'reconciling with words' becomes far more dynamic - more than just words in fact. The words are transformed into things that intensify and thereby empower one's sense of self - both my own and my client's.

Look at your Pluto Keyphrase - and now feel it as a source of power in the form of a water main. While pondering your Pluto Keyphrase, imagine what the water pressure from this main feels like. When you have felt this to your satisfaction - which means that you experience it as a physical sensation, a vivid image or a powerful emotion - comment on your experience:

This feels like a bodily function that I only have limited control over. It is powerful and must have a healthy outlet.

cont'd

Example PROFILING MARS & PLUTO ALLIANCE Lyn cont'd

Now send sensation, image or emotion down an imaginary hose which has a nozzle at the end which is presently *closed*. This nozzle is Mars. Note: If you find yourself not able to experience this sensation, image or emotion, then you are not ready to receive Pluto's pressure. So cease this exercise and come back to it another time if you wish. Just note if you are able, or not, to experience this in some way, and receive Pluto's pressure:

Able.

Having done this look at your Mars Keyphrase again and with this firmly in mind open the nozzle and notice what you see or feel shooting out from it. Comment on this Experience:

I feel my word power being affirmed. A very positive sensation.

Now, having released this Plutonian pressure in the form of your Mars Keyphrase, be aware of what kind of feeling or sensation goes back down the hose to the main. Describe this sensation:

This is a release of pressure, so a commensurate degree of comfort returns to my physical and emotional bodies. This is healthy.

Focus on how the 'main' experiences this feeling of release of pressure and expression of its power. Describe:

Indeed, as a release, as already noted above. There is a degree of satisfaction overall, but also the awareness that I just have to find a verbal (or otherwise) expression of this Pluto power, or it could build up and become troublesome.

Once more look at your Pluto Keyphrase and place the feeling evoked by it in your abdomen just below your navel, storing it there for when you next need to access your power from the main. Describe this Experience or Sensation:

Simply empowering.

♂♇ PROFILING MARS & PLUTO ALLIANCE

PLANET	SIGN	HOUSE
MARS		
PLUTO		

Comment on how you see these two Keyphrases side by side, on how they combine:

Look at your Pluto Keyphrase - and now feel it as a source of power in the form of a water main. While pondering your Pluto Keyphrase, imagine what the water pressure from this main feels like. When you have felt this to your satisfaction - which means that you experience it as a physical sensation, a vivid image or a powerful emotion - comment on your experience:

cont'd

♂♇ *PROFILING MARS & PLUTO ALLIANCE* cont'd

Now send sensation, image or emotion down an imaginary hose which has a nozzle at the end which is presently *closed*. This nozzle is Mars. Note: If you find yourself not able to experience this sensation, image or emotion, then you are not ready to receive Pluto's pressure. So cease this exercise and come back to it another time if you wish. Just note if you are able, or not, to experience this in some way, and receive Pluto's pressure:

Having done this look at your Mars Keyphrase again and with this firmly in mind open the nozzle and notice what you see or feel shooting out from it. Comment on this Experience:

Now, having released this Plutonian pressure in the form of your Mars Keyphrase, be aware of what kind of feeling or sensation goes back down the hose to the main. Describe this sensation:

cont'd

♂♀ *PROFILING MARS & PLUTO ALLIANCE* cont'd

Once more look at your Pluto Keyphrase and place the feeling evoked by it in your abdomen just below your navel, storing it there for when you next need to access your power from the main. Describe this Experience or Sensation:

Once more look at your Pluto Keyphrase and place the feeling evoked by it in your abdomen just below your navel, storing it there for when you next need to access your power from the main. Describe this Experience or Sensation:

Take a deep breath or two and ponder on the whole of the above Exercise.

Jupiter & Saturn

The Management

We now enter the Realm of Society, that mixture of both individual and collective forces which we are all, to varying degrees, subject to and governed by. We now encounter *The Management* and discover how much you are doing the managing or how much you are being managed by someone or something else.

In Exercises 4 to 12 we were concerned with Profiling three planetary pairs – Mercury/Uranus, Venus/Neptune and Mars/ Pluto – which are each made up of a lower and a higher octave. But now we have reached two Planets, the largest in our Solar System, which are also a pair, but not in the sense of lower octave/inner planet/personal and higher octave/outer planet/ transpersonal. Jupiter and Saturn are positioned between these two poles of Inner Planets (Mercury, Venus & Mars) and Outer Planets (Uranus, Neptune and Pluto), and as such it could be said that they are the *social* Planets in the sense of being an amalgamation of both personal and transpersonal forces. And so, whether this appears to come from without or from within, these forces can be seen as an *opportunity* (Jupiter) or as a *test* (Saturn) with regard to attaining a better life and also to safely entering those transpersonal realms that are the domain of the Outer Planets.

In other words, all that is symbolized by Jupiter and Saturn is both a product of us as individual beings, and also of what is created by us, which is that entity called *culture* and *society*, with its *laws* and *customs* (Jupiter), and with its *boundaries* and *governance* (Saturn). And in turn, this entity, *The Management*, influences us as individuals, and so on and so forth.

In Profiling Jupiter and Saturn it therefore needs to be borne in mind that, initially at least, the qualities that they represent won't be entirely up to you as to how you shape them. It will at first be a case of how they have shaped you. We are all born into a certain type of society with its cultural and living standards, its religious persuasions, its national heritage, its political environment, etc. So you might create a Keyphrase that you like to think is entirely up to you and about you – but on reflection its nature and realization may be seen, to a greater or lesser extent, **as** being conditioned by ideas and attitudes that were put in place at a stage when you had little or no say in the matter. Your Keyphrases should also tell you about that.

Yet at the same time, creating your Jupiter and Saturn Keyphrases can show you how to make the influences of these two Planets all or mostly your own, and not just experience them as something that is 'managing' *you*.

Many if not all people seek to 'go up in the world' in the sense of *increasing* (Jupiter) and/or *establishing* (Saturn) themselves within the system/management in which they find themselves. In order to do so they have to play by the rules and dictates of that system, as well as taking advantage of whatever it has to offer.

Then again, it needs to be stated that *The Management* is ultimately only managing us in so far as we allow it to do so. This is because the call of the Outer Planets urges us to revolutionize or be free of (Uranus) the system, to transcend or escape from it (Neptune), and in the end to transform or destroy it, or be destroyed by it (Pluto). It could be argued that such liberation, transcendence and transformation has to be accomplished primarily in oneself and one's own individual life before one sets about changing the world. At any rate, *The Management* can be seen as something that has got power over the individual – but which progressively becomes less and less so as one *seeks* (Jupiter) and *builds* (Saturn) something called 'self-management'. Self-management may well be the key to an ultimately healthy self-governing society, an enlightened anarchy even.

So to sum up, Jupiter is symbolic of something that is *ever-growing* whereas Saturn is symbolic of something that is *ever-stabilizing* – both in the context of the Sign and House positions of these two Planets. Importantly, they should be seen as *compensating* for one another. Jupiter left to its own devices, without the *limiting* influence of Saturn, can become too *expansive* with the result of unwanted or unhealthy growth, an *excess* of something, *inflation, spending beyond one's means*, etc. Saturn left to its own devices, without the *enterprising* and *adventurous* influence of Jupiter, can become too *cautious* and become *rigid, stuck, worn-out, austere* and *fearful*.

Most significantly, Jupiter's sense of growth gives rise to *faith*, and Saturn's sense of stability gives rise to *order*. But one without the other can give rise to *over-optimism* in the first case, and to *doubt* and *decrepitude* in the second. In this context Jupiter and Saturn can be seen as two very important polarities: the *Divine* (Jupiter) and the *Secular* (Saturn). Therefore Jupiter gives rise to *conceptualizing* and *opinions* whereas Saturn comes down to *realizing* (making real) and *hard facts*.

As pointed out previously, Saturn is termed a *Malefic* planet as it has a great potential to produce negative emotions and states. Jupiter, by virtue of the all-important Law of Compensation, is (along with Venus) one of the *Benefics* – producing *joyful* and *positive* states. For similar reasons Jupiter is symbolic of *good fortune* because such is born of a sense that everything is *developing* in accordance with some unifying purpose, in the same way that individual body cells know what organ they are growing into. But it is Saturn which knows the *structure* of that 'organ', without which such good fortune would become only so much *hot-air, impractical promise* or worse.

So you may now begin by Profiling JUPITER and then proceed when ready to Profiling SATURN as you did with the other planetary pairs before this.

As ever, you may find it advantageous to *Profile both* before

158

you complete or offer up just the one of them. This is because you will most likely find how the Profiling of the one affects your Profiling of the other. This means that you may find that you need to edit what you have done for Jupiter after compensatory promptings felt through doing Saturn – and vice versa.

Exercise 13 - Profiling Jupiter

The questions or assignments are initially what you yourself answer and perform, and subsequently what you can apply to others.

1. In the table below headed ♃ *PROFILING JUPITER*, following the *Example*, insert the position of JUPITER by SIGN and HOUSE (as given in your chart) in the third row in the relevant columns. *Enter name top-right.*

2. From the **Primary Dynamic Keywords** on page 251 freely select **one** keyword each for JUPITER, SIGN and HOUSE and then insert them in the fourth row in the appropriate columns as in the *Example* below. You now have your Jupiter Keyphrase on the fourth row, which for our Example of William Blake is plainly: "I Seek to Explore Self-Expression."

Example		*William Blake*
PLANET	SIGN	HOUSE
JUPITER	*Sagittarius*	*5th*
Seeking	*To Explore*	*Self-Expression*

Important Note – As Jupiter takes almost 12 years to orbit the Sun, the energies or qualities of its Sign position apply to a one year-long generation, the time it takes for it to transit one Sign. This means that the Jupiterian energies of Enjoying, Growing and Seeking apply themselves to matters regarding that Sign. So in our *Example*, William Blake was not only part of a Jupiter in Sagittarius generation that was "Seeking to Explore" – or whatever Keyphrase you choose for this Planet/Sign position – but he also personally expressed his Jupiterian generational qualities, firstly through its House position (the 5th) and then with the 'assistance' of the other planetary energies in the rest of his birth chart – that is, of his personality as a whole. In his case, he made the Seeking to Explore Self-Expression very much something of his own, and in so doing he actually contributed to his culture, then and up until the present day, in the form of his writings and paintings.

♃ PROFILING JUPITER:		
PLANET	SIGN	HOUSE
JUPITER		

3. When you have done the above to your satisfaction, answer the following questions, referring to the appropriate Keyword Clouds beginning on page 257 if you feel the need to jog your mind, enhance meaning or stimulate your imagination.

Jupiter Questions

☺ *If you cannot answer any question come back to it later.*

a) Record or write down freely the feelings, thoughts and impressions that you experience on reading and pondering your Jupiter Keyphrase.

b) What character traits would you say were evidence or expressions of your Jupiter Keyphrase?

c) What events, situations or feelings, if any, would you say are a testament to your being true to your Jupiter Keyphrase?

d) What events, feelings or situations, if any, would you say are a testament to your NOT being true to your Jupiter Keyphrase? How could you move on through or out of such situations in order to embody or realize your Jupiter Keyphrase?

e) What does your Jupiter Keyphrase tell you about your idea or image of, or belief in, a Deity – like a God or Goddess – in the sense of something divine that is overseeing or managing things from 'above' or 'below' or 'within' or wherever? What is your relationship to this Deity? NOTE: If you have no such image or belief, then see this *as* your belief, e.g. agnosticism is itself a belief, rather than a fact, as there is nothing to either prove or disprove the existence of a Deity. How does all this relate to the religion in which you were or were not brought up, and/or in which you were educated? Expand and reflect.

f) Have there been any religious or 'divine' moments (an epiphany even) in your life, particularly early on? How does this bear on your Jupiter Keyphrase?

g) Does your Jupiter Keyphrase incline you towards an optimistic/positive outlook or a pessimistic outlook? As a consequence of this, in what way has this contributed or not to your benefiting from good fortune? Hint: Take a step back and consider in what ways positive events have occurred in your life without you actually having done anything, or have occurred as a result of your own good deeds or acts of faith – especially in relation to your Jupiter Keyphrase (and check out different House keywords in the House Keyword Clouds to jog your memory to this end).

h) What are you growing or growing into, especially but not entirely in the context of your Jupiter Keyphrase? Expand.

i) *"... all shall be well and all manner of things shall be well,"* said the anchoress Julian of Norwich in the 14/15th century. If you knew with utter certainty that what she said was and is true, how would it change your life, and in particular how would it change your interpretation of your Jupiter Keyphrase – or change your Keyphrase altogether? What could you do to give yourself an ongoing reminder of Julian's pronouncement? And most importantly, what does your Saturn (Keyphrase) have to say about it?

j) In what way or ways is the promise of your Jupiter Keyphrase affected by the nature of your Saturn Keyphrase? (You will have to do your Saturn Keyphrase now if you haven't already.)

k) Make a summing up statement concerning all of the above. Doing this will reveal to you how through using *Dynamic Interactive Astrology* you are becoming not only versed in astrology, but becoming more aware of yourself as a unique individual. Feel free to share parts of your Summary Statement in the *Dynamic Interactive Astrology Facebook Group* at: www.facebook.com/groups/dynamicinteractiveastrology

Additional Jupiter Exercises

It is recommended that having completed the above, you do it all again, now or later, choosing another set of Dynamic Keywords to make a different Jupiter, Sign and House Keyphrase.

This gives you another slant on the chart/person's dynamics and characteristics.

You can repeat this with alternative keywords as many times as you like or see fit. You can also refer to the relevant Keyword Clouds on page 263 for extra, sometimes more advanced, keywords.

Exercise 14 - Profiling Saturn

The questions are initially what you yourself answer and perform, and subsequently what you can apply to others.

1. In the table below headed ♄ *PROFILING SATURN*, following the *Example,* insert the position of SATURN by SIGN and HOUSE (as given in your chart) in the third row in the relevant columns. *Enter name top-right.*

2. From the **Primary Dynamic Keywords** on page 251 freely select **one** keyword each for SATURN, SIGN and HOUSE and then insert them in the fourth row in the appropriate columns as in the *Example* below. You now have your Saturn Keyphrase on the fourth row, which for our Example of Nelson Mandela is unequivocally: "(My) Authority Commands (my) Culture."

Example		*Nelson Mandela*
PLANET	SIGN	HOUSE
SATURN	*Leo*	*9th*
Authority	*To Command*	*Culture*

Important Note – As Saturn takes 29.5 years to orbit the Sun, the energies or qualities of its Sign position apply to a 2-3 year-long generation, the time it takes for it to transit one Sign. This means that the Saturnian energies of Authority, Learning and Necessity apply themselves to matters regarding that Sign. So in our *Example,* Mandela was not only part of a Saturn in Leo generation that was about the "Authority to Command" – or whatever Keyphrase you choose for this Planet/Sign position – but he also personally expressed his Saturnian generational qualities firstly through its House position (9th), and then with the 'assistance' of the other planetary energies in the rest of his birth chart – that is, of his personality as a whole. In his case, he earned the Authority to Command his Culture in a very hard and testing way typical of Saturn. He also Structured (Saturn) a Rule (Leo) of Law (9th) that desegregated South Africa as a country.

♄ *PROFILING SATURN:*		
PLANET	SIGN	HOUSE
SATURN		

3. When you have done the above to your satisfaction, answer the following questions, referring to the appropriate Keyword Clouds beginning on page 257 if you feel the need to jog your mind, enhance meaning or stimulate your imagination.

Saturn Questions

☺ *If you cannot answer any question come back to it later.*

a) Record or write down freely the feelings, thoughts and impressions that you experience on reading and pondering your Saturn Keyphrase.

b) What character traits would you say were evidence or expressions of your Saturn Keyphrase?

c) What events, situations or feelings, if any, would you say are a testament to your being true to your Saturn Keyphrase?

d) What events, feelings or situations, if any, would you say are a testament to your NOT being true to your Saturn Keyphrase? How could you move on through or out of such situations in order to embody or realize your Saturn Keyphrase?

e) Saturn is the Planet of Time – Old Father Time, with his scythe and hourglass. How do you view your Saturn Keyphrase in the context of time passing, of how long things take to learn or accomplish, and of using time as your instrument or feeling against the clock?

f) Saturn is called the Lord of Karma in that it keeps the karmic score and metes out lessons which we need to learn resulting from past acts of commission or omission. What does your Keyphrase tell you about possible karmic dues you are paying or have paid in the form of something? For example, a relationship that is or was very difficult could be one form taken of paying off such karmic dues.

g) Saturn is the Planet that governs the dense material plane, along with the Law of Gravity which keep us all bound to that plane. If you feel weighed down or that life is just too much effort it is possibly because you are not fully living out your Saturn Keyphrase – or even because you are not living it out gladly, something which could be supplied by your Jupiter Keyphrase. Explore these suggestions.

h) In what way or ways is the objective of your Saturn Keyphrase affected by the nature of your Jupiter Keyphrase? (You will have to do your Jupiter Keyphrase now if you haven't already.)

i) Saturn has a negative reputation of being the Planet of (1) hardship, (2) misfortune, (3) denial and (4) austerity. But this is invariably a consequence of (1) taking it too easy, (2) omitting to perform some duty, (3) needing to learn some lesson before one can move on, or (4) spending more than one can afford. And all of these issues have one thing behind them: FEAR. (1) Fear of making an effort for fear of failing; (2) Fear of getting it wrong; (3) Fear of taking things step by step because of impatience, which is simply a poor sense of Time – see question (e) above; or (4) Fear of being seen to be lacking whereas Saturn is largely about lack as a preface and pressure to earn and achieve and thereby realize one's Saturn Keyphrase, and also to get one's Jupiter in gear. Reflect and comment on all of the above where they have a bearing on your Saturn Keyphrase in particular, and on your thoughts and feelings about Saturnian issues and necessities generally.

j) Saturn is the Planet of Authority. Ultimately it is about assuming and building one's own sense of authority through being the 'author' of one's own life. Along the way though, we are subject to the authority of others – parents, teachers, officials, government, etc. – and it could be said that the degree of such subjection to the authority of others is relative to how much you are being your own authority through learning and achieving what your Saturn is telling you, beginning with your Keyphrase. Comment.

k) Make a summing up statement concerning all of the above. Doing this will reveal to you how through using *Dynamic Interactive Astrology* you are becoming not only versed in astrology, but becoming more aware of yourself as a unique individual. Feel free to share parts of your Summary Statement in the *Dynamic Interactive Astrology Facebook Group* at: www. facebook.com/groups/dynamicinteractiveastrology

Additional Saturn Exercises

It is recommended that having completed the above, you do it all again, now or later, choosing another set of Dynamic Keywords to make a different Saturn, Sign and House Keyphrase. This gives you another slant on the chart/person's dynamics and characteristics.

You can repeat this with alternative keywords as many times as you like or see fit. You can also refer to the relevant Keyword Clouds on page 264 for extra, sometimes more advanced, keywords.

Exercise 15 - Profiling Jupiter & Saturn
Balance of Power

This is a tool and an Exercise that serves to heighten your sense of what these two Planets mean to you, and how they feel to you. This enables you to resonate with Jupiter and Saturn in your own and others' birth charts. Getting to know *The Management* means that you become better at managing to live healthily and successfully in the midst of the experiences that astrological influences symbolize. In particular this can be greatly assisted by understanding how to balance the effects of these, the two biggest planets in our Solar System, and to always consider them as being in tandem.

First of all, through the use of a metaphor, we explain below how *The Management* operates. As you read this you will see certain *italicized words*. Whenever this is the case, equipped with what you have learnt through Profiling these two Planets, note down between the brackets {following the *italicized word*} whether you think it is Jupiter or Saturn that rules or represents the meaning of each of these words. You can then check the 'answers' at the end of this section. Scan or photocopy this part of the Exercise for multiple use.

Example: "And with *joy* {Jupiter}
we'll *persevere* {Saturn}"

You are a physical being. Much as this statement seems obvious, we tend to forget what being physical actually means. One of the most important aspects of physical existence is pressure. We can appreciate this by thinking of an automobile tire. The tire itself has an internal air pressure to counteract the external air pressure of our atmosphere. When the internal pressure is too low or too high in relation to the external pressure then this affects the vehicle in certain ways while travelling.

Relating all this to being human is quite simple. We travel around, or live, with an internal sense of life and ourselves. This 'internal pressure' is what we need in order to respond to and contend with the pressures of living in the world of people and things, the 'external pressure'.

In the context of this metaphor, we can say that *Jupiter represents the internal pressure*, while *Saturn stands for the external pressure*. And you cannot, and should not, consider the one without the other. When your internal pressure or *faith* {_____} in yourself and life is too low then the external pressures or *demands* {_____} of our daily lives become too hard to bear and eventually can even crush us or put us 'off the road'.

Alternatively, when our internal pressure is too high or we have an *inflated* {_____} idea of our capabilities and prospects, and through ignoring the *limitations* {_____} placed on us by the external pressure (which includes your physical body) we can *burn-out* {_____}. Alternatively, external pressure has to compensate in some way like, for instance, causing us to run afoul of someone in *authority* {_____}, which includes anyone who has an emotional hold on us.

The tire metaphor again applies here in that with lower tire pressure it is more *stable* {_____} as there is more *grip* {_____} on the road surface (like for wet weather driving) but it uses up more energy – or when far too low causes the vehicle to grind to a halt – and so *limits* {_____} how far we can go. With higher tire pressure there is less grip and less energy used, but driving is more *risky* {_____} as there is far less *control* {_____} over the vehicle (you, that is), especially if an emergency or the unexpected should happen.

The principle of pressure can also be seen in terms of something highly applicable to our own physical health and existence: blood pressure. With *low blood pressure* {_____} we feel weak and faint, so, psychologically speaking, we need *pumping up* {_____} with a stronger sense of ourselves in order to cope with life. This can also mean feigning humility (being a victim) in order to avoid asserting oneself. With *high blood pressure* {_____} we are *overcompensating* {_____} for what we feel the pressures of the outside world to be – and so need to calm down, or be let down. This could also mean appearing to be *full of oneself* {_____} as a *defense mechanism* {_____}.

Answers

joy - faith - inflated - burn-out - risky - pumping up - high blood pressure - overcompensating - full of oneself {all **Jupiter**}

    persevere - demands - limitations - authority - stable - grip - limits - control - low blood pressure - defense mechanism {all Saturn}

The Glyphs

All of the above can actually be seen in the original symbols or glyphs for Jupiter and Saturn. Both are comprised of two other symbols: the Crescent for the Moon and the Cross for Matter. The Moon represents, as you know, your emotional being, that is, your personal sense of existing. So, Jupiter, on the left, the Crescent on top of the Cross, is the personal, emotional sense taking precedence over the material world and its pressures and considerations. Saturn, on the right, has those material pressures and considerations taking precedence over your emotional or personal state of being.

The Jupiter-Saturn Balance of Power

On the following two pages is a table of various states or problems experienced through having either too much Saturn and not enough Jupiter, or the reverse, along with the remedies that they can be met with. It is recommended that you add your own problems and remedies if or when they occur to you. NOTE – The problems can result from compensation, that is, too much Jupiterian behavior can eventually attract more Saturn influences in to your life, or conversely, too much Saturnian behavior will attract more Jupiter influences. For example, high blood pressure (too much Jupiter) could be a condition compensating for feeling inhibited (too much Saturn).

Please feel free to share your responses or findings on the *Dynamic Interactive Astrology Facebook Group* at: www.facebook. com/groups/dynamicinteractiveastrology

♄ TOO MUCH SATURN and NOT ENOUGH JUPITER	♃ JUPITER REMEDY Of the below, adopt one or more that appeals to you or applies to one or more of the problems described on the left
♄ Feeling sluggish and/or depressed. ♄ Feeling intimidated by life and others. ♄ A sense of hopelessness. ♄ Lacking in confidence . ♄ Fearfulness. ♄ Worry and anxiety. ♄ Low Blood Pressure.	♃ Cultivate optimism; look on the bright side; accentuate the positive, attenuate the negative. Laugh - a sense of humour is a sense of proportion. ♃ Fill your life with a faith in someone or something, yourself, or a higher being. Follow your dreams. ♃ Be more assertive and ebullient. Be theatrical, outgoing and larger than life. ♃ Attract joy into your life by being true to your promises, exercising understanding, and protecting the sanctity of your inner being (Moon). ♃ Do yogic breathing exercises. This literally 'pumps' you up, filling you with the spirit of enthusiasm - *pneuma*, as in pneumatic, is the Greek for 'spirit' or 'breath of life'. ♃ Acquire a philosophy of life than enables you to see the bigger picture, thereby cutting your perceived problems down to size or putting them into a more meaningful perspective. ♃ Be more adventurous; feel the fear and do it anyway. Get out, do something different. Let experience be your teacher rather than worry be your tormentor. ♃ Be more open and spontaneous; have less agendas and rigid expectations. ♃ Take vigorous physical exercise, let off steam, have a good scream and shout.

♃ TOO MUCH JUPITER and NOT ENOUGH SATURN	♄ SATURN REMEDY Of the below, adopt one or more that appeals to you or applies to one or more of the problems described on the left
♃ Over-optimism giving rise to deflation or not being taken seriously by others ♃ Over-commitment; promising more than you can deliver. ♃ Excessiveness and indulgence, giving rise to health or weight problems, lack of control and wasted time and energy. ♃ False confidence created by alcohol, drugs, delusions of grandeur, etc. ♃ Licence giving rise to lack of discipline. ♃ High Blood Pressure.	♄ Give yourself readily achievable goals, rather than pie-in-the-sky projects. ♄ Ask yourself why you are trying to please or impress others more than yourself. Make the distinction between what you expect of yourself and what you have been led to believe others expect of you (but probably do not). ♄ Remember that actions speak louder than words. DO IT, don't just think about it. Walk your talk. ♄ Practice the Art of Humility. True greatness veils itself. ♄ By your works shall they know you – not by your intentions. ♄ Identify the 'gap' in your life that you are trying to fill, and then you will know how to successfully fill it. This would be 'creatively indulging' yourself. ♄ Channel excessiveness into a productive pursuit to benefit yourself *and* others. ♄ Use your time constructively – draw up a plan and schedule and KEEP TO IT. ♄ Become aware of how you overreact to/overcompensate for what you feel to be inadequacies, rather than being clear what those actual shortcomings are. ♄ Take up a program of exercise, study or relaxation – preferably one involving others that make sure you stay the course. ♄ Give actuality to words of wisdom.

Ascendant/Descendant & Midheaven/ Lower Midheaven

The Cross You Bear

We now engage with *The Cross You Bear*, which is comprised of what are called the *Angles* of the birth chart. The Houses depict, as you know, the experiences we encounter during our lives on planet Earth. The Angles are the cusps (the beginnings and so most sharply defined areas of Houses) of the four most important Houses, the *Angular* Houses: 1st, 4th, 7th and 10th. These Angles or Angular House cusps are called respectively: Ascendant, Lower Midheaven (now more usually referred to as the IC, see below, but I prefer to keep its verbal description, in keeping with the other three Angles), Descendant, and Midheaven. In brief, these represent respectively: Self + Inner Life + Others + Outer Life = *The Cross You Bear*.

This chapter is divided into two halves; the first is concerning the Horizontal Axis of the 'Cross', the second is about the Vertical Axis.

The Horizontal Axis – Ascendant/Descendant

The astrological Houses, of which this Horizontal Axis is possibly the most important part, are probably what the beginner finds hardest to grasp so, if needs be, while doing these Exercises refer to 'The Astrological Houses – A Pictorial Diagram' on page 197. The Houses are actually termed the 'Mundane Houses' as they tell us in what worldly areas of experience all that planetary energy is expressed, felt and manifested. To calculate the Houses in a birth chart it is necessary to know one's birth time as they are determined by this (and one's birth place).

The Horizontal Axis, also sometimes called the Horizon of Consciousness, is simply the Southern Horizon which is the horizontal line that bisects the chart wheel on your birth chart. (In the southern hemisphere it would actually be the northern horizon, but it is an astrological convention to have south at the top and north at the bottom.) The Ascendant, abbreviated to **AS**, is the Point at which the horizon intersects the Zodiac to the far left, that is, in the East (when looking southwards). The Descendant, abbreviated to **DS**, is where the horizon intersects the Zodiac to the far right, that is, in the West (again, when looking southwards). The Vertical Axis, to be explained and explored shortly, has the following abbreviations: Midheaven as **MC** (Medium Coeli – *middle of the sky*) and Lower Midheaven as **IC** (Imum Coeli – *bottom of the sky*).

As the Ascendant – the Sign on which is called the Rising Sign – is where the Signs and Planets rise, it symbolizes an *emerging into consciousness*. This is the event/experience called *birth*. So the Ascendant symbolizes not only the nature of your birth, your coming into the world, but also how you continue to *present* yourself to it. It is your *presence, image* and *character*. It is your *self* and your *identity*. It is your *first impression*, given and received. As the Houses represent the experiences of life, the 1st House is therefore the primary experience, that of the experienc*er*, for without him or her there would no other experiences! For this reason, the 1st House is probably the most important of all the Houses.

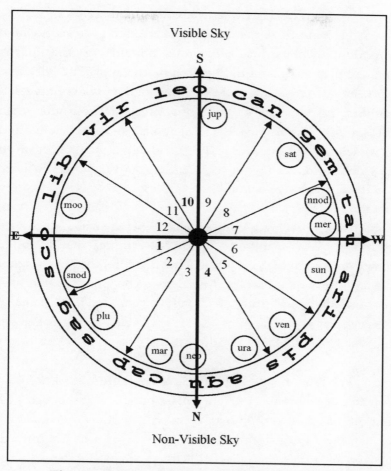

The Astrological Houses - A Pictorial Diagram

As the Earth rotates within the Zodiac band, the House Cusps (arrowed lines) all move *anti-clockwise* through all twelve Signs of the Zodiac, once in one day, like the spokes of a wheel (House numbers are indicated around centre of chart). The Planets are moving, at their individual speeds, progressively through the Signs, *also* in an *anti-clockwise* direction (except the Nodes, which travel backwards). The Planets are seen to rise in the East, set in the West, etc., apparently going in a *clockwise* direction, because the Earth/House Cusps are rotating *faster* than the Planets are travelling through the Signs. Note1.Cardinal points correspond to the Angles as follows: E=AS; W=DS; N=IC; S=MC. Note 2.Chart is drawn up for Full Moon on April 16th 2003 at 20.40 BST London. Note 3.All positions are approximated for the sake of illustration.

The True Significance of Image

In our age in particular, 'image' is enormously, even excessively, important. Things like glamorous advertising and plastic surgery play a big part in the modern image-making business. And the current fashion of 'selfies' – photos taken of oneself with a handheld device – kind of says it all! The trouble with this kind of 'importance' is that it can cause superficiality and shallowness, and interior qualities and values go unrecognized and undeveloped. If you look good then everything will be alright, right? But as any 'fading star' finds out, this is inevitably not the case.

Astrology, however, makes it clear what the true significance of image is. In so doing it also reveals things that are quite magical about human existence. First and foremost it states that we are *born* with an image. And this image, although it is seen primarily to be physical in terms of looks and manner, it is also energetic or psychical. This will be revealed as we look further into the Ascendant and Profile it.

What You Put Out Equals What You Get Back

A major part of that 'magic' just mentioned is that the image we put out has a powerful, distinct and mostly unconscious effect on what we get back from life and the world in the form of *others* and our *relationships* with those others, the very things that the *De*scendant, at the other end of the Horizontal Axis, symbolizes. The Sign on the Descendant is the Setting Sign. The image we project could be said to actually create what we get back, as surely as the film that goes through a projector creates what we get on the screen. Simply put, the Ascendant and Descendant are ganged together in the same way that there is no east without there being a west. This phenomenon of 'Self' determining what 'Other' you attract into your life will also be revealed as you Profile your Descendant.

Profiling the Ascendant and Descendant

As ever, you may find it advantageous to Profile both before you complete or finalize just the one of them. This is because you will most likely find how the Profiling of the one affects your Profiling of the other. This means that you may find that you need to edit what you have done for the Ascendant after compensatory promptings felt through doing the Descendant – and vice versa.

Ruling Planets – During or after Profiling take note that Planets which are said to *rule* the Ascendant and Descendant (according to their Signs) exert extra influence over, and give more information about, your image/persona and relating/ relationships, respectively. Some schools of thought deem the Ruler of your Ascendant/Rising Sign as ruling the chart/personality as a whole, while others prefer to select a significantly placed Planet as the chart Ruler, while still others do not entertain the idea of an overall chart Ruler at all. For the beginner, the first option is probably best. To determine what Planet rules your Rising and Setting Signs refer to the **Primary Dynamic Keywords** page 251. Where a Sign has a 'secondary ruler' regard its influence as having a secondary effect. *Example:* an Aquarius Ascendant has Uranus as its ruler, and Saturn as its secondary ruler. Having ascertained Rulers you can then refer to your Profiles of the Planets concerned to add a further dimension to the significance of your Ascendant and Descendant.

Exercise 16 - Profiling Ascendant/Descendant

The questions or assignments are initially what you yourself answer and perform, and subsequently what you can apply to others.

1. In the table on page 202 headed *AS PROFILING ASCENDANT / DS PROFILING DESCENDANT*, following the *Example*, insert the position of the ASCENDANT by SIGN in the third row in the right-hand column. (Note there is no House position for the Ascendant as it is itself the cusp of the 1st House.) *Enter name top-right.*

2. Now Profile the exactly *opposite Point* to this, which is the DESCENDANT. So look at the Birth Chart to identify the Sign opposing the Ascendant, which will be on the far right of the horizontal line. Refer to 'The Astrological Houses – A Pictorial Diagram' above, if need be. Alternatively, find on your birth chart where it is actually written what the Sign on your Ascendant is and work out the opposite Sign from the following pairs of opposite Signs which will reveal your Descendant Sign: Aries<>Libra; Taurus<>Scorpio; Gemini<>Sagittarius; Cancer<>Capricorn; Leo<>Aquarius; Virgo<>Pisces. Then insert it in the fifth row and in right-hand column as in the *Example* below.

3. From the **Primary Dynamic Keywords** freely select **one** keyword each for the ASCENDANT and its SIGN, and then insert them in the fourth row in the appropriate columns as in the *Example* below. Then do the same for the DESCENDANT and its SIGN, inserting the keywords in the sixth row in the appropriate columns, again as in the *Example* below.

Example	*Margaret Thatcher*
POINT	SIGN
ASCENDANT	*Scorpio*
Image	*To Influence*
DESCENDANT	*Taurus*
Other	*To Stabilize*

Important Note: If there are any Planets in the 1st House this will strongly affect your persona and image in addition to what the Ascendant Sign indicates. Similarly, if there are any Planets in the 7th House this will have a definite influence on the nature of partners and relationships in addition to what the Descendant Sign indicates. So in such cases, take this firmly into account. In the case of our *Example*, Margaret Thatcher had Saturn in her 1st House (actually in the 12th but *conjoined to the Ascendant* which makes it even more '1st House', hence her nickname, the 'Iron Lady', although 'Leaden Lady' would also have been appropriate as Saturn rules lead, while Mars, her Scorpio Ascendant's Secondary Ruler, rules iron).

Reminder: What you put out equals what you get back. From here, as you do this Profiling remember that these two important Points in a birth chart are ganged together because what you express as your persona and what immediate impressions you give and get (Ascendant) all come back as an opposing, complementary or balancing energy in the form of an Other (Descendant), that is, partner, opposite number, better half, adversary, shadow, or other people's responses in general. In the *Example* above, Denis, Margaret Thatcher's husband, was actually a Taurus Sun, the Sign on her Descendant, and was known to be a stabilizing influence.

AS *PROFILING ASCENDANT:* DS *PROFILING DESCENDANT:*	
POINT	SIGN
ASCENDANT	
DESCENDANT	

4. When you have done the above to your satisfaction, answer the following Questions, referring to the appropriate Keyword Clouds in the Toolkit on page 257 if you feel the need to jog your mind, enhance meaning or stimulate your imagination. NOTE for Ascendant consult the First House Keyword Cloud, and for Descendant use the Seventh House Cloud. Keyword Clouds also broaden your knowledge of astrological symbolism and correspondences generally.

If you feel like going back to a previous question to add

or change something, please feel free to do so. And freely associating and exploring meanings at length also helps the revelatory process.

The questions that follow are all *specific* to the ASCENDANT/ DESCENDANT axis.

Ascendant/Descendant Questions
☺ *If you cannot answer any question come back to it later.*

a) How do you see your Ascendant Keyphrase as helping you to present or express what is important to you, in the present and the past? Is your 'image' matched by your 'product', and vice versa?

b) Who in your life has a strong emphasis (like Sun, Moon, Ascendant or a number of Planets) in your Ascendant Sign and comment on how they have affected the expression of your Ascendant Keyphrase?

c) In what way, if any, is your image or persona, as described by your Keyphrase, possibly restricting or giving a limited or inaccurate impression of who you are as a whole individual? How could you move on through or out of such situations in order to use your Ascendant Keyphrase rather than it use you?

d) What relationships or significant others, if any, would you say are a testament to their being true to your Descendant Keyphrase? If you know a partner's or an adversary's astrological makeup, you may include here any emphasis (like Sun, Moon, Ascendant or a number of Planets) that they have in your Descendant Sign as evidence of the statement: "What you give out equals what you get back" factor.

e) Consider your Ascendant Keyphrase as describing what you project as an emanation or light-beam on to other(s) – reselect keywords that are more suitable if you wish or need to. Now using your Descendant Keyphrase as a descriptor or clue, what is it telling you about the *shadow* your Ascendant/light-beam is casting on other(s) in the form of some trait of character of your own that you have been led to believe is negative or 'not you'? Then reconsider how such a shadow is actually your 'other half' and would, if owned, complete you, give you a facet of being that would suit you, empower you, make you more whole.

f) How do you see your Descendant Keyphrase as helping you to relate and/or attract a mate, in the present and the past? Conversely, in what ways does it make, or has it made, such relating and attracting difficult? Explore and compare. BIG TIP: Study the keywords of your Descendant Sign and then try acting out some of them with a significant other and they will begin to relate to you more positively. This is because you are consciously projecting at them the qualities of your shadow which means that they then relate to you positively, more appropriately, because they no longer have to act out your shadow unconsciously/negatively.

g) Determine the Ruling Planet(s) of your Ascendant and by consulting your Profile(s) for that Planet or those Planets, factor what they say into the context and meaning of your Ascendant that you have established so far.

h) Determine the Ruling Planet(s) of your Descendant and by consulting your Profile(s) for that Planet or those Planets, factor what they say into the context and meaning of your Descendant that you have established so far.

i) Make a summing up statement concerning all of the above. Doing this will reveal to you how through using *Dynamic Interactive Astrology* you are becoming not only versed in astrology, but becoming more aware of yourself as a unique individual. Feel free to share parts of your Summary Statement in the *Dynamic Interactive Astrology Facebook Group* at: www.facebook.com/groups/dynamicinteractiveastrology

Additional Exercise

It is recommended that having completed the above, you do it all again, now or later, choosing another set of Dynamic Keywords to make different Ascendant and Descendant Keyphrases.

This gives you another slant on the chart/person's dynamics and characteristics.

You can repeat this with alternative keywords as many times as you like or see fit. You can also refer to the relevant Keyword Clouds for extra, sometimes more intermediate or advanced keywords.

Completing Core Blend

Back in Exercise 3, on page 35, you profiled the Sun & Moon Blend which is two parts of something called the Core Blend, with the third part being the Ascendant, which you have just Profiled.

In that Exercise we called the Sun & Moon Blend "the engine that powers your very existence". Now we add the Ascendant to this as being the *product* or *expression* of that engine. Or we could say that the Sun is the 'Father', the Moon is the 'Mother', and the Ascendant is their 'Child'. So, with our Example of Oprah Winfrey we profiled her 'engine' as follows:

Example PROFILING SUN & MOON BLEND		*Oprah Winfrey*
MOON KEYPHRASE	ACTION	SUN KEYPHRASE
Instinct to Develop Foundations	Feeds or Drives	*Purpose to Liberate Self-Expression*

Now add the Ascendant Keyphrase as the Child or Product of the above. Oprah having her **Ascendant in Virgo**, gives a Keyphrase of:

Image to Improve or Improving Self

This could be said to be the ultimate product of her Sun &
Moon Blend – completing her Core Blend. Now do the same
for yourself or whomever, using your Sun & Moon Blend from
Exercise 3 and your existing or a new Ascendant Keyphrase.

On the next page we continue to engage with *The Cross You
Bear*, which as described above is comprised of what are called
the *Angles* of the birth chart. This time we look at and Profile the
Vertical Axis.

The Vertical Axis – Midheaven/Lower Midheaven

The Vertical Axis, also sometimes called the Axis of Power, is the Meridian which is the more or less vertical line that bisects the chart wheel on your birth chart. Actually the further one is born from the equator the more it will vary from vertical. The Midheaven or **MC** (Medium Coeli – *middle of the sky*) is the Point at which the Meridian intersects the Zodiac at the top, the Zenith or where the Sun would be at midday. The Lower Midheaven or **IC** (Imum Coeli – *bottom of the sky*) is where the Meridian intersects the Zodiac at the bottom, the Nadir or where the Sun would be at midnight.

As the Midheaven is where the Signs and Planets reach their highest point in the sky, it symbolizes *recognition* and an amounting to something in the world. So the Midheaven shows the way in which we may *achieve* and *succeed materially* in the *outer world*. Although it can sometimes actually describe the nature of one's *profession, status* or *public image* itself, it is probably more helpful to see it in terms of *how* one becomes a success or makes some headway in the world over and above *what* it is that one is successful at or holds a position in. For example, Midheaven in Aries is more likely to indicate that one has to *fight* to get somewhere rather than it necessarily saying that one would actually be a fighter of some kind, although one might well be. It is also very useful to view the Midheaven as symbolizing or describing your *life mission*.

The Importance of Roots

When considering the other, bottom end of the Vertical Axis, the IC or Lower Midheaven, inasmuch as a building is only as good as its foundations, any position achieved in the outer world is ultimately only as good as what underpins it in the form of basic *security* and a sense of *belonging*. Whereas the Midheaven urges us to reach for the sky, the Lower Midheaven urges us to keep *rooted* in our *private* and *family* life, and ultimately in our *origins*

215

and *Nature* herself. The Sign on one's Lower Midheaven can therefore describe the way in which we are connected and can connect with these fundamentals of *foundation*, including *Mother Earth* herself. It also depicts the qualities which compensate for what it takes to function or succeed in the external world. For example, the Aries Midheaven individual just described would have their Lower Midheaven in the opposite Sign of Libra, indicating that a haven of harmony and beauty is where they'd like to come *home* to at night after a day battling for success and recognition. Again, as with the Midheaven and profession, the Lower Midheaven can actually describe the nature and atmosphere of one's home, roots, family, etc. according to its Sign position.

Profiling the Midheaven and Lower Midheaven
As ever, you may find it advantageous to Profile both before you complete or finalize just the one of them. This is because you will most likely find how the Profiling of the one affects your Profiling of the other. This means that you may find that you need to edit what you have done for the Midheaven after compensatory promptings felt through doing the Lower Midheaven – and vice versa.

Ruling Planets – During or after Profiling take note that Planets which are said to *rule* the Midheaven and Lower Midheaven (according to their Signs) exert extra influence over, and give more information about, the nature and means of attaining status/professional recognition and of your roots/domestic security, respectively. To determine what Planets rule the Signs on your Midheaven and Lower Midheaven refer to the **Primary Dynamic Keywords** on page 251. Where a Sign has a 'secondary ruler' regard its influence as having a secondary effect. *Example:* Scorpio Midheaven has Pluto as its ruler, and Mars as its secondary ruler. Having ascertained Rulers you can then refer to your Profiles of the Planets concerned to add a further dimension to the significance of your Midheaven and Lower Midheaven.

Exercise 17 - Profiling Midheaven/Lower Midheaven

The questions or assignments are initially what you yourself answer and perform, and subsequently what you can apply to others.

1. In the table on page 220 headed **MC PROFILING MIDHEAVEN / IC PROFILING LOWER MIDHEAVEN**, following the *Example*, insert the position of the MIDHEAVEN by SIGN in the third row in the right-hand column. (Note there is no House position for the Midheaven as it is itself the cusp of the 10th House.) *Enter name top-right.*

2. Now Profile the exactly *opposite Point* to this, which is the LOWER MIDHEAVEN. So look at the Birth Chart to identify the Sign opposing the Midheaven, which will be at the bottom end of the more or less vertical line, which often has an arrow at the top end. Refer to 'The Astrological Houses – A Pictorial Diagram' on page 197. Alternatively, find on your birth chart where it is actually written what the Sign on your Midheaven/ MC is and work out the opposite Sign from the following pairs of opposite Signs which will reveal your Lower Midheaven/ IC Sign: Aries<>Libra; Taurus<>Scorpio; Gemini<>Sagittarius; Cancer<>Capricorn; Leo<>Aquarius; Virgo<>Pisces. Then insert it in the fifth row and in the second column as in the *Example* below.

3. From the **Primary Dynamic Keywords** on page 251, freely select **one** keyword each for the MIDHEAVEN and its SIGN, and then insert them in the fourth row in the appropriate columns as in the *Example* below. Then do the same for the LOWER MIDHEAVEN and its SIGN, and then insert their relevant keywords in the sixth row in the appropriate columns, again as in the *Example* below.

Example	*Queen Elizabeth II*
POINT	SIGN
MIDHEAVEN	*Scorpio*
Status	*To Influence*
LOWER MIDHEAVEN	*Taurus*
Origins	*To Stabilize*

Important Note: If there are any Planets in the 10th House this will strongly affect your public image and what it takes to achieve success in addition to what the Midheaven indicates. Similarly, if there are any Planets in the 4th House this will have a definite influence on the nature of your home/private life and roots in addition to what the Lower Midheaven Sign indicates. So in such cases take this firmly into account. In the case of our *Example*, Queen Elizabeth II has Saturn in her 10th House (actually in the 9th but *conjoined* to the Midheaven which makes it even more '10th House' which lends weight, authority and longevity to her worldly position). Also note how Queen Elizabeth has the 'Status to Influence' (MC in Scorpio) whereas Margaret Thatcher has the 'Image to Influence' (AS in Scorpio – see previous Exercise).

Reminder: 'How' more than 'what'. Remember that the Signs on the Midheaven and Lower Midheaven primarily describe *how* one may, or has to, achieve material position or success in the first case, or attain security and a sense of belonging in the second case. So it could help to insert a link phrase, e.g. MC in Aries = *(for) Recognition (it is necessary) to Fight.* The actual nature of either may or may not be described by the Sign position, particularly regarding the Midheaven.

MC *PROFILING MIDHEAVEN:*
IC *PROFILING LOWER MIDHEAVEN:*

POINT	SIGN
MIDHEAVEN	
DESCENDANT	

4. When you have done the above to your satisfaction, answer the following Questions, referring to the appropriate Keyword Clouds if you feel the need to jog your mind, enhance meaning or stimulate your imagination. NOTE: for Midheaven consult the Tenth House Keyword Cloud; for Lower Midheaven use

the Fourth House Cloud. Keyword Clouds also broaden your knowledge of astrological symbolism and correspondences generally.

If you feel like going back to a previous Question to add or change something, please feel free to do so. And freely associating and exploring meanings at length also helps the revelatory process.

The Questions that follow are all *specific* to the MIDHEAVEN/ LOWER MIDHEAVEN axis.

Midheaven/Lower Midheaven Questions
☺ *If you cannot answer any question come back to it later.*

a) How much, and in what ways, would you say material or professional achievement in your life has been aided, or could be aided, by following the dictates of your Midheaven Keyphrase?

b) Who in your life has a strong emphasis (like Sun, Moon, Ascendant or a number of Planets) in your Midheaven Sign and comment on how they affect or have affected the expression of your Midheaven Keyphrase and your career advancement?

c) In what ways, if any, has the nature of your Midheaven Keyphrase made it difficult for you to advance professionally and/or achieve recognition? Consider how you could change this by exploring how you feel about your Keyphrase or choosing different keywords to make it up.

d) How much, and in what ways, has your private life, roots and domestic security been aided, or could be aided, by following the prescription of your Lower Midheaven Keyphrase? In what ways does your Keyphrase describe the nature of your home and origins?

e) In what ways, if any, has the nature of your Lower Midheaven Keyphrase made it difficult for you to find a good home base and a sense of belonging? Consider how you could change this by exploring how you feel about your Keyphrase or choosing different keywords to make it up.

f) Study your Midheaven and Lower Midheaven Keyphrases with the former placed above the latter and consider how the two are or could be related, ganged together or interdependent. For example, in the context of your Keyphrases, how does the quality of your roots or home life feed the flowering of your profession or status? In other words, what would the experience of your being out in the world need in the form of somewhere to come home to and recharge your batteries? Conversely, what do you strive for out in the world in order that you might bring home what is needed there. In other words, and generally speaking, how does one compensate for, or benefit from, the other?

g) Determine the Ruling Planet(s) of your Midheaven and by consulting your Profile(s) for that Planet or those Planets, factor what they say into the context and meaning of your Midheaven that you have established so far.

h) Determine the Ruling Planet(s) of your Lower Midheaven and by consulting your Profile(s) for that Planet or those Planets, factor what they say into the context and meaning of your Lower Midheaven that you have established so far.

i) Make a summing up statement concerning all of the above. Doing this will reveal to you how through using *Dynamic Interactive Astrology* you are becoming not only versed in astrology, but becoming more aware of yourself as a unique individual. Feel free to share parts of your Summary Statement in the *Dynamic Interactive Astrology Facebook Group* at: www. facebook.com/groups/dynamicinteractiveastrology

Additional Exercise

It is recommended that having completed the above, you do it all again, now or later, choosing another set of Dynamic Keywords to make different Midheaven and Lower Midheaven Keyphrases.

This gives you another slant on the chart/person's dynamics and characteristics.

You can repeat this with alternative keywords as many times as you like or see fit. You can also refer to the relevant Keyword Clouds for extra, sometimes more intermediate or advanced keywords.

The Lunar Nodes

The Trends

We now encounter the two Nodes of the Moon – the North Node and the South Node – which represent, respectively, what you are becoming, and, what you were. I have dubbed these *The Trends* as they indicate, especially in a karmic sense, what is IN or OUT regarding the direction your life is supposed to take. Physically, the Nodes are where the Moon's orbit around the Earth intersects the ecliptic (the apparent path of the Sun around the Earth) in a Northerly direction, and directly opposite, in a Southerly direction.

As for how we are viewing 'karma' here, rather than getting confused by various schools of thought, let's look at it energetically.

Everything, including you and I, is energy. Energy is never born and never dies, it just keeps changing form. So the energy that is you has a history – your 'energy history' – which determines the form it takes in any particular life. This is your karma.

The North Node, which is also called the Dragon's Head, can be likened to the conditions and traits that comprise the furrow you are advised, or rather obliged, to *plough* in this life. Another way of understanding this is to see your soul as a boat voyaging through the seas of time. The North Node/Dragon's Head is like the *prow* of your little soul boat, pushing against the water, *making headway* and *progress*, creating and *cultivating capacities*, while leaving the past with its bad habits and inappropriate attitudes progressively behind – but naturally *encountering resistance*. As a Karmic Trend it is IN, which means to say it is the *new direction* that leads towards your *destiny*, that being the direction in which your life fundamentally wants to go according to some program deep within your psyche.

Following your destiny *optimizes the flow of events* in your life as it helps you avoid going down blind alleys and false trails, even though sometimes doing so may be a necessary part of discovering your destiny.

The South Node, which is also called the Dragon's Tail, can be likened to where you came from, the conditions and traits that comprised your *past* – whether you think of that as being of this life or of previous lives – and which have become ingrained in your personality as *old patterns*, for good or ill. So again using the soul boat analogy, the South Node/Dragon's Tail is the *stern* of that boat, with its *wash* forever leaving behind or *phasing out predispositions* born of where you have been and who you were in the sense of what has become *outmoded* or even *obstructive to progress*. As a Karmic Trend it is OUT. However, in effect you can never let go of it entirely as it is the stern of a boat that lends stability and enables one to steer. So it is also your *store of talents* born of both positive and negative experiences, indicating where you need to *conserve abilities* and make the most of them.

Sometimes you may see contradictions where something is IN as well as OUT, but this would mean that in this present lifetime or stage of this life a quality of personality which is OUT is still particularly important and valuable, or needs working out and cleaning up before you can steam ahead towards your destiny.

Profiling the North Node and South Node

As ever, you may find it advantageous to Profile both before you complete or finalize just the one of them. This is because you will most likely find how the Profiling of the one affects your Profiling of the other. This means that you may find that you need to edit what you have done for the North Node after compensatory promptings felt through doing the South Node – and vice versa.

Ruling Planets – During or after Profiling take note that Planets which are said to *rule* the North Node and South Node (according to their Signs) exert extra influence over, and give more information about, your Karmic Trends, IN and OUT respectively. To determine what Planets rule the Signs of your North Node and South Node refer to the **Primary Dynamic Keywords** on page 251. Where a Sign has a 'secondary ruler' regard its influence as having a secondary effect. *Example:* a Pisces North Node has Neptune as its ruler, and Jupiter as its secondary ruler. Having ascertained Rulers you can then refer to your Profiles of the Planets concerned to add a further dimension to the significance of your North Node and South Node.

Exercise 18 - Profiling Lunar Nodes

The Questions are initially what you yourself answer and perform, and subsequently what you can apply to others.

1. In the table on page 237 headed ☊*PROFILING NORTH NODE* / ☋*PROFILING SOUTH NODE*, following the *Example*, insert the position of the NORTH NODE by SIGN and HOUSE in the third row in the relevant column. To do this, you will need to find on your Birth Chart where it is written what the Sign and House of your North Node is. *Enter name top-right.*

2. Now Profile the exactly *opposite Point* to this, which is the SOUTH NODE. Unless it is also written on your Birth Chart, to do this you work out the opposite Sign from the following pairs of opposing Signs which will reveal your South Node Sign: Aries<>Libra; Taurus<>Scorpio; Gemini<>Sagittarius; Cancer<>Capricorn; Leo<>Aquarius; Virgo<>Pisces. So if your North Node was in Aquarius then your South Node would be in Leo, and vice versa. Now work out the opposite House from these pairs of opposing Houses: 1st<>7th; 2nd<>8th; 3rd<>9th; 4th<>10th; 5th<>11th; 6th<>12th. So if your North Node was in 1st House then your South Node would be in the 7th, and vice versa.

Alternatively, you could look at the actual chart wheel on your Birth Chart to identify the Sign and House opposing the North Node, possibly with the help of referring to 'The Astrological Houses – A Pictorial Diagram' on page 197, where the North Node is in Taurus in the 7th House and the South Node in Scorpio in the 1st House. However, this method can be a little unreliable as the positions of the Nodes are not always that clear graphically. They are best determined from the written data.

When you have discovered the Sign and House of your SOUTH NODE insert them each in the fifth row in the appropriate columns as in the *Example* below.

3. From the **Primary Dynamic Keywords** freely select **one**

keyword each for the NORTH NODE, its SIGN and its HOUSE, and then insert in the fourth row in the appropriate columns as in the *Example* below. However, as the SOUTH NODE has to do with where you need to *conserve the ability* and draw from *as well as* what you are having to *progressively leave behind*, you are given two rows (6 and 7) into which you enter keywords for the SOUTH NODE, its SIGN and its HOUSE as they apply to both the former and to the latter, as shown in the *Example* below. TIP: Consult the South Node *SIGN* Keyword Cloud to further identify any negatives regarding habits and patterns of behavior that need to be left behind.

Example		*Aleister Crowley**
POINT	SIGN	HOUSE
NORTH NODE	*Aries*	*9th*
Cultivating the Capacity	*To Fight (for)*	*Beliefs*
SOUTH NODE	*Libra*	*3rd*
Conserving he Ability	*To Beautify*	*(with) Words*
Phase Out Predispositions	*To Please*	*Everyday Thinking*

The choice of keywords here is naturally quite personal, so it has been assumed what Crowley's choices might have been in the light of his works, personal history and reputation. He never let social opinion get in the way of his beliefs and putting them into practice (to put it mildly!), and he was, and still is, recognized as a writer with an original and rich literary style.

☊ *PROFILING NORTH NODE:* ☋ *PROFILING SOUTH NODE:*		
POINT	SIGN	HOUSE
NORTH NODE		
SOUTH NODE		

4. When you have done the above to your satisfaction, answer the following Questions. If you feel like going back to a previous question to add or change something, please feel free to do so. And freely associating and exploring meanings at length also helps the revelatory process.

North Node/South Node Questions

☺ *If you cannot answer any question come back to it later.*

a) Expand on what your Keyphrase for your North Node means to you.

b) Expand on what your Keyphrase for your South Node means to you.

c) What character traits, activities and situations in your life would you say were positive expressions of your North Node Keyphrase in that they are taking your life in the right direction?

d) What character traits, activities and situations in your life would you say were positive expressions of your South Node Keyphrase in that they indicate innate abilities?

e) What character traits, activities and situations in your life would you say were negative expressions of your South Node Keyphrase, *as given in the seventh row*, in that they tend to hold you back, give you trouble, or have a retro feeling about them – especially with regard to how they might impede your North Node Keyphrase? Consider how you may actively phase out such components.

f) Who do you know that has any emphasis (like Sun, Moon, Ascendant or a number of Planets) in the same Sign as your North Node? What do they tell you or show you about your North Node Keyphrases, that is, the meaning and symbolism of the North Node in your life?

g) Who do you know that has any emphasis (like Sun, Moon, Ascendant or a number of Planets) in the same Sign as your South Node? What do they tell you or show you about both your positive/conserving and negative/phasing out South Node Keyphrases, that is, the meaning and symbolism of the South Node in your life?

h) Determine the Ruling Planet(s) of your North Node and by consulting your Profile(s) for that Planet or those Planets, factor what they say into the context and meaning of your North Node that you have established so far.

i) Determine the Ruling Planet(s) of your South Node and by consulting your Profile(s) for that Planet or those Planets, factor what they say into the context and meaning of your South Node that you have established so far. Include both the positive/conserving and negative/outmoded dimensions.

j) Combine the Keyphrase of your North Node (as entered on the fourth row) with the two Keyphrases of your South Node (as entered on the sixth and seventh rows) in order to arrive at a more complete sense of your destiny's direction or bearing, and ease or difficulty with which it can be achieved.

k) Make a summing up statement concerning all of the above. Doing this will reveal to you how through using *Dynamic Interactive Astrology* you are becoming not only versed in astrology, but becoming more aware of yourself as a unique individual. Feel free to share parts of your Summary Statement in the *Dynamic Interactive Astrology Facebook Group* at: www.facebook.com/groups/dynamicinteractiveastrology

Additional Exercise

It is recommended that having completed the above, you do it all again, now or later, choosing another set of Dynamic Keywords to make different North Node and South Node Keyphrases.

This gives you another slant on the chart/person's dynamics and characteristics.

You can repeat this with alternative keywords as many times as you like or see fit. You can also refer to the relevant Keyword Clouds for extra, sometimes more intermediate or advanced keywords.

Toolkit

Primary Dynamic Keywords*
The Keyword Clouds*
Chart 'A' Explained
*Scan/Photocopy for Ease Of Use
And Remember...
Planets Shine through Signs and Live in Houses
Turn the Keywords and Enter the Meaning

Primary Dynamic Keywords For Planets, Points, Signs & Houses

How To Use The Tables (on following pages)

Depending on what you are looking up, go to the relevant table for Planet, Point, Sign or House Keywords. Find the Planet, Point, Sign or House you are Profiling and pick the Keyword(s) of your choice from the ones given beneath it. The first keyword for each Planet, Point, Sign or House – given in **bold** lettering – is possibly the best all round keyword, e.g. SUN is **'Purpose'**. However, it is very important that you pick the Keywords which appeal to you personally.

Each Planet, Point, Sign and House is denoted as follows:

Planet Keywords

At the top of each individual cell the Planet is first denoted by its *glyph* and then by its name as the first three letters in CAPitals.

Point Keywords

At the top of each individual cell the Point is first denoted by either an abbreviation of two capitalized letters, or an actual *glyph*, followed > by its actual name.

Sign Keywords

At the top of each individual cell the Sign is first denoted by its *glyph* and then by its name as the first three letters in CAPitals. This is followed by the *glyph* of its Ruling Planet and then by a *glyph*, in a smaller font, of its Secondary or Co-Ruler, *if* it has one. This last point is explained in the relevant Profiling text.

House Keywords

At the top of each individual cell the House is denoted by its verbal Number. This is followed by the *glyph* of its corresponding Sign, which is in turn followed by the *glyph* of its corresponding Ruling Planet and its Secondary or Co-Ruler, *if* it has one.

Link-Words

Use these examples, and those of your own making, between Sign and House Keywords:

to - through - under - in - on - off - over - by - from - with - against - leads to - producing - type of - by interacting with

Also

Change parts of speech, tense, etc. to enliven, make Keyphrases more coherent and meaningful.

PRIMARY DYNAMIC *PLANET* KEYWORDS	
☉ **SUN** **Purpose** Confidence Life-Force	☽ **MOOn** **Need** Caring Instinct
☿ **MERcury** **Communicating** Perceiving Thinking	♅ **URAnus** **Awakening** Changing Precipitating
♀ **VENus** **Beauty/Attracting** Art/Charming Socializing/Love	♆ **NEPtune** **Sensitizing** Attuning Inspiring
♂ **MARs** **(Sex) Drive** Effectiveness Go-Getting	♇ **PLUto** **Empowering** Intensifying Transforming
♃ **JUPiter** **Growing** Enjoying Seeking	♄ **SATurn** **Necessity/Time** Authority Learning/Effort

PRIMARY DYNAMIC *POINT* KEYWORDS

AS > Ascendant **Persona/Image** Birth/Presence/Self Window on World	**DS > Descendant** **Other(s)/Adversaries** Relating/Relationship Shadow/Life's Mirror
MC > Midheaven **Mission/Profession** Achievement/Status Succeeding /Recognition	**IC > Lower Midheaven** **Home/Private/Inner life** Roots/Origins Nature/Earth Link
☊ > North Node **New Direction/Destiny** Cultivating the Capacity Encountering Resistance	**☋ > South Node** **Old Patterns (pos. & neg.)** Conserving the Ability Phase Out Predispositions

PRIMARY DYNAMIC *SIGN* KEYWORDS

♈ ARI ♂	**♎ LIB ♀**
To Win (over)/Lead/Sell	**To Harmonize/Please**
To Fight (for)/Compete	To Arbitrate/Reconcile
To Make Happen	To Beautify/Grace
♉ TAU ♀	**♏ SCO ♇♂**
To Stabilize/Substantiate	**To Empower/Influence**
To Relish/Delight	To Authenticate/Merge
To Value/Own	To Penetrate/ Deepen
♊ GEM ☿	**♐ SAG ♃**
To Communicate	**To Explore/Enthuse/Seek**
To Amuse/Inform	To Grow/Develop/Believe
To Facilitate	To Teach/Further
♋ CAN ☽	**♑ CAP ♄**
To Feel/Receive	**To Build/Achieve**
To Nurture/Comfort	To Mature
To Sympathize	To Organize
♌ LEO ☉	**♒ AQU ♅♄**
To Command/Rule/Create	**To Reform/Liberate**
To Dramatize/Entertain	To Befriend/Detach
To Express/Illuminate	To Research/Distance
♍ VIR ☿	**♓ PIS ♆♃**
To Improve	**To Inspire/Transcend**
To Analyze/Purify	To Accept/Surrender
To Serve/Help	To Heal/Suffer/Relieve

PRIMARY DYNAMIC *HOUSE* KEYWORDS

FIRST ♈♂	**SEVENTH** ♎♀
Presence/Persona	**Relationship/Partner**
Self/Image	Adversaries/Shadow
Window-on-the-World	Others/Life's Mirror
SECOND ♉♀	**EIGHTH** ♏♇♂
Self-Worth/Talents	**Intimacy/Crisis/Soul**
Money/Substance	Astral/Occult Realms
Resources/Earnings	Transformation/Death
THIRD ♊☿	**NINTH** ♐♃
Communication/Words	**Beliefs/Culture/Laws/Divinity**
Education/Thinking	Education(Higher)/Philosophy
Everyday Life/Mindset	Far Journeys/Foreign Affairs
FOURTH ♋☽	**TENTH** ♑♄
Home/Private/Inner Life	**Material Success/Mission**
Foundations/Family	Authority/Status
Roots/Nature/Security	Public Image/Recognition
FIFTH ♌☉	**ELEVENTH** ♒♅♄
Creations/Fun/Sex	**Social Values/Politics**
Self-Expression/Play	Friends/Groups
Speculation/Children	Media/Networking
SIXTH ♍☿	**TWELFTH** ♓♆♃
Health (bodymind)/Work	**Karma/Womb Life/Source**
Methods/Training/Coaching	Behind-the-Scenes/Unseen
Co-workers/Pets	Retreat/Meditation/Institutions

The Keyword Clouds

These also give negative meanings, which allow you to identify any negative expressions and transmute them into the positive.

Where possible, space is given in each cloud to add Keywords that you discover to be also relevant as you become more versed in astrological symbolism and correspondences.

Planet & Point Keyword Clouds - Index

[1]For Ascendant Keywords see First House Keywords on page 274

[2]For Descendant Keywords see Seventh House Keywords on page 276

[3]For Midheaven Keywords see Tenth House Keywords on page 277

[4]For Lower Midheaven Keywords see Fourth House Keywords on page 275

Planet & Point Keyword Clouds

SUN KEYWORD CLOUD

Acting   Actor   Aristocrat   Backbone   Bragging   Celebrating

Centre   Centre-of-Attention   Conceit   Confidence   Creating

Dignity   Ego(tism)   Entertaining   Fame   Father   Gambling

Giving   Glory   Gold   Heart   Hero   Identifying   Illuminating

Importance   King   Life   Life-Force   Light   Lord   Male

Pride   Prince   Purpose   Radiating   Ruling   Shining   Spine

Spirit   Star   Vitality   Will

MOON KEYWORD CLOUD

Belonging   Bias   Breasts   Care   Caring   Child(hood)

Clannishness   Clinging   Comfort   Comforting   Conceiving

Defensiveness   Domesticating   Dream   Empathizing

Familiarizing   Family   Feelings   Female   Fertility   Fluctuating

Food   Fruitfulness   Habit   Heroine   Home   Homemaking

Inclination   Instinct   Memory   Mood   Mother   Nature   Need

Nourishment   Nurturing   Over-Reacting   Past   Phases

Predisposition   Princess   Protecting   Queen   Race   Reacting

Receptivity   Reflecting   Responding   Safety   Security

Sentiment   Smothering   Soul   Spoiling   Support   Survival

Sympathy   Unconscious   Womb   Welcoming

MERCURY KEYWORD CLOUD

Agent Alertness Anxiety Arms Breathing Calculating

Clerk Cleverness Commenting Communicating Connecting

Contacting Critic Curiosity Dabbling Deduction Dexterity

Differentiating Dodger Editing Educating Guide Hands

Imitating Informing Inquiring Insomnia Intellect(ualizing)

Interviewing Journalism Listening Literature Lower-Mind

Lungs Mentoring Merchandizing Messaging Messenger

Nerves Perceiving Persuading Quickening Rationalizing

Reasoning Replicating Secularizing Senses Smartness

Speaking Swiftness Thinking Translating Travelling Vehicle

Verbalizing Villain Wired Wit Words Work Writing

Youth

VENUS KEYWORD CLOUD

Admiring Adorning Affection Agreeing Amorousness

Appealing Appreciating Attracting Art Artist Attraction

Beautifying Beauty Charming Delighting Embellishing

Eroticizing Fancying Fashion Femininity Flowering Gift

Girl Gratifying Harmonizing Indulging Lazing Liking

Love Lover Loving Money Ornament Pleasing Pleasure

Pleasuring Poise Relating Relaxing Satisfying Sensuality

Singing Smiling Socializing Style Styl(iz)ing Suiting

Superficiality Sweetening Taste Teasing Toying Treating

Value(s) Valuing Vanity Voice Worth

MARS KEYWORD CLOUD

Acting   Actualizing   Advancing   Affronting   Aggression   Anger

Ardour   Arming   Asserting   Attacking   Blood   Boy   Brutality

Burning   Challenging   Championing   Competing   Conflict

Conqueror   Courage   Danger   Daring   Deciding   Desire

Disputing   Dissenting   Doing   Drive   Effectiveness

Endangering   Exercising   Exerting   Fever   Fighting   Forcing

Go-getting   Hard-hitting   Heat   Hostility   Hunting   Inflaming

Irritating   Leading   Masculinity   Militarizing   Pioneering

Promoting   Pursuing   Pushing   Questing   Raw-Energy   Redness

Selfishness   Selling   Sex-Drive   Sharps   Strife   Striving

Suitor   Tools   Violence   Wanting   War   Weapons   Wooing

262

JUPITER KEYWORD CLOUD

Abundance   Academia   Acquiring   Adventuring   Advertising

Believing   Benefiting   Benevolence   Bigger-Picture

Broadcasting   Concept   Culture   Customs   Developing

Dogmatizing   Divine   Emphasizing   Enjoying   Enterprising

Enthusing   Exaggerating   Excelling   Excessiveness   Expanding

Faith   Furthering   Gallantry   Giving   Glory   God   Goddess

Godparent   Good-Fortune   Grandparent   Gratitude   Greatness

Growing   Honesty   Horses   Increasing   Indoctrinating   Inflating

Joy   Judging   Justice   Largesse   Legislating   Luxuriating

Managing   Morality   Opportunity   Opinion   Optimism

Overdoing   Preaching   Paradigm   Philanthropy   Philosophy

Pilgrimage   Praying   Preaching   Priest   Priestess   Proliferating

Promising   Prophesying   Providence   Publicizing   Religion

Roaming   Seeking   Superiority   Temperance   Understanding

Wandering   Wasting   Wisdom

SATURN KEYWORD CLOUD

Affliction   Aging   Apathy   Assessing   Austerity   Authority

Bearing   Blocking   Borders   Boundaries   Building   Caution

Coldness   Conforming   Containing   Contracting   Controlling

Decrepitude   Denying   Despairing   Difficulty   Discipline

Doubting   Duty   Efficiency   Effort   Elder   Enduring

Establishing   Facts   Fearing   Freezing-out   Governing   Gravity

Guaranteeing   Guilt   Hesitating   Inadequacy   Inhibiting

Judging   Learning   Limiting   Managing   Materialism   Maturing

Measuring   Misfortune   Mistrusting   Misusing   Necessity

Order(ing)   Organizing   Persevering   Pragmatism   Pressuring

Prohibiting   Reality   Realizing   Reducing   Restricting   Retiring

Rigidifying   Secular   Slowing-down   Sobriety   Stabilizing

Structuring   Stuck   (The) System   Testing   Time   Trusting

Utilizing

URANUS KEYWORD CLOUD

Aborting   Accidents   Alien   Altering   Alternative   Astrology

Awakening   Chance   Changing   Computing   Convulsing

Defying   Detaching   Disaster   Disrupting   Divorcing

Eccentricity   Electrifying   Engineering   Evolving   Experimenting

Exploding   Flying   Fool   Freedom   Future   Genius

Individuation   Informality   Innovating   Intuition   Inventing

Liberating   Magic   Metaphysics   Modernity   Now   Oddness

Originality   Outsider   Out-of-the-Blue   Paradox   Pathfinding

Pituitary   Precipitating   Psychology   Randomness   Rebelling

Reforming   Resisting   Revolting   Revolutionizing   Science

Shocking   Spasm   Stars   Surprising   Symbols   Synchronizing

Technology   Truth   Uniqueness   Unpredictability   Unusualness

Upgrading   Whirling

NEPTUNE KEYWORD CLOUD

Addicting   Astral-travelling   Attuning   Accepting   Bacteria

Chaos   Channel   Christ   Clouds   Coma   Collective-Unconscious

Compassion   Confessing   Confusing   Conscience   Dancing

Deceiving   Devas   Dissolving   Divining   Dreaming   Drugging

Ecstasy   Escaping   Fantasizing   Fascinating   Film   Flooding

Flowing   Flushing-out   Forgiving   Ghosts   Healing

Hypnotizing   Hysteria   Idealizing   Illusion   Imagining

Infatuating   Insanity   Inspiring   Intoxicating   Inundating

Longing   Meditating   Metaphor   Mind-Altering   Music

Mystery   Mysticism   Oneness   Peace   Photography   Poetry

Psychic   Redeeming   Releasing   Sacrificing   Sailing   Saviour

Sea   Selflessness   Sensiti-vity/zing   Sleep-inducing   Sleeping

Softening   Spiritualizing   Suffering   Surrendering   Undermining

Uplifting   Vagueness   Victimhood   Viruses   Vision   Weakening

Weeping

PLUTO KEYWORD CLOUD

Ancient Anus Authenticity Betraying Bowels Compulsion
Concentrating Corrupting Crisis Darkness Death Decaying
Deepening Dogs Eliminating Eliminating-Outworn
Empowering Evil Extremism Fanatic Fate Garbage
Genitals Hidden Horror Insight Intensifying Intimacy
Merging Monster Obsession Occult Parasites Penetrating
Perverting Power Primordial Psychologizing Purging
Putrefying Raping Re(birth) Regenerating Reptile Rubbish
Ruthlessness Scandalizing Secrecy Secretiveness Sexuality
Shaman Shame Spying Stalking Taboos Thoroughness
Transforming Underworld Vampirism Vice Waste Wealth

ASCENDANT KEYWORDS

See First House Keyword Cloud on page 274

DESCENDANT KEYWORDS

See Seventh House Keyword Cloud on page 276

MIDHEAVEN KEYWORDS

See Tenth House Keyword Cloud on page 277

LOWER MIDHEAVEN KEYWORDS

See Fourth House Keyword Cloud on page 275

LUNAR NODES KEYWORD CLOUDS

NORTH NODE or DRAGON'S HEAD

Cultivate-Capacities   Destiny   Evolving-towards

Encountering-Resistance   Karmic-Trend-IN   New-Direction

Making-Headway-and-Progress   Optimize-Flow-of-Events   Plough

Prow

SOUTH NODE or DRAGON'S TAIL

Conserve-Abilities   Evolving-away-from   Karmic-Trend-OUT

Obstructive-to-Progress   Old-Patterns   Outmoded   Past

Phase-Out-Predispositions   Progressively-Leave-Behind   Stern

Store-of-Talents

Sign Keyword Clouds

ARIES KEYWORD CLOUD

Act   Activate   Actualize   Champion   Compete   Courageously

Directly   Do   Endanger   Fight-for   Force   Hard-Sell

Impatiently   Impetuously   Impulsively   Independently   Insist

Lead   Make-Happen   Over-Simplify   Push   Quest   Sell

Simplify   Straightforwardly   Strive   Want   Win-over

TAURUS KEYWORD CLOUD

Craft   Cultivate   Delight   Densely   Indulge   Laze   Maintain

Materialistically   Own   Persevere   Ponder   Possess   Produce

Refuse   Relish   Sensually   Sing   Slowly   Stabilize   Steady

Stubbornly   Substantiate   Treasure   Trudge   Value   Withhold

GEMINI KEYWORD CLOUD

Amuse   Bodge   Communicate   Connect   Curiously   Dabble

Deliver   Diversify   Dodge   Easily   Facilitate   Gossip   Inform

Inquire   Interest   Learn   Mimic   Rationalize   Rationalize-Away

Read   Secularize   Skim   Split   Talk   Think   Trivialize   Write

CANCER KEYWORD CLOUD

Accommodate   Brood   Bury   Care   Cater   Comfort   Conceive

Domesticate   Dream   Feed   Feel   Gestate   Indirectly   Mother

Nurse   Nurture   Over-Protect   Over-React   Protect   React

Receive   Respond   Secure   Sulk   Sympathize   Smother

LEO KEYWORD CLOUD

Affirm   Ascertain   Assure   Boast   Command   Confidently

Create   Dignify   Dominate   Dramatize   Ennoble   Entertain

Express   Father   Flatter   Give   Illuminate   Palpitate   Patronize

Perform   Play   Radiate   Romanticize   Rule   Stage

VIRGO KEYWORD CLOUD

Analyze   Criticize   Decline   Demur   Discriminate   Distil

Draft   Edit   Exact   Fret   Heal   Help   Improve   Perfect

Prepare   Purify   Resolve   Serve   Study   Train   Withdraw

Work   Worry

LIBRA KEYWORD CLOUD

Accompany   Adorn   Ally   Arbitrate   Balance   Beautify

Compromise   Elegantly   Fashion   Grace   Harmonize   Justice

Like   Nicely   Please   Prevaricate   Reconcile   Refine   Relate

Superficially   Vacillate   Weigh-up

SCORPIO KEYWORD CLOUD

Authenticate   Blackmail   Cloak   Coerce   Conceal   Convince

Deepen   Delve   Desire   Destroy   Disempower   Eliminate

Empower   Hurt   Influence   Intensify   Intimate   Merge   Obsess

Penetrate   Poison   Secrete   Seduce   Sexually   Sexualize

Transform

SAGITTARIUS KEYWORD CLOUD

Advertise   Believe   Confront   Develop   Enthuse   Envision

Excessively   Expand   Experience   Explore   Further   Gallop

Generously   Grow   Honour   Horse-around   Indulge   Judge

Mock   Moralizing   Overdo   Philosophize   Preach   Religiously

Run   Teach   Travel   Zealous

CAPRICORN KEYWORD CLOUD

Achieve   Bear   Build   Climb   Condition   Conform   Control

Endure   Establish   Govern   Limit   Mature   Order   Organize

Patriarchy   Preside   Restrict   Set   Suppress   Use

AQUARIUS KEYWORD CLOUD

Befriend   Blank   Civilize   Co-operate   Cryptically   Democratize

Detach   Distance   Equalize   Humanize   Innovate   Liberate

Over-Tolerate   Paradoxically   Politicize   Reform   Refresh

Research   Theorize   Tolerate   Uniquely   Unusually

PISCES KEYWORD CLOUD

Accept   Addict   Camouflage   Compassionately   Confuse

Delude   Dissolve   Elude   Empathize   Enchant   Escape   Falsify

Fascinate   Give-Up   Heal   Imitate   Inspire   Obscure   Relieve

Sabotage   Sacrifice   Sensitize   Soothe   Spiritualize   Subtly

Suffer   Surrender   Tempt   Transcend   Undo   Veil

House Keyword Clouds

FIRST HOUSE KEYWORD CLOUD

Appearance   Attitude   Beginning   Birth   Character   Demeanour

Early-environment   Emergence   Eyes   First-Impression   Identity

Image   Looks   Persona   Physical-Body   Presence   Self

Window-on-the-World

SECOND HOUSE KEYWORD CLOUD

Accounts   Bank   Earning-power   Finances   Income

Material Value   Money   Ownership   Productivity   Property

Quality   Resources   Self-worth   Shopping   Storage   Substance

Talents

THIRD HOUSE KEYWORD CLOUD

Breathing   Commerce   Communication   Education   Errands

Everyday-life   Everyday-thinking   Everyday-world   Humour

Information   Journalism   Knowledge   Lower-Education   Mindset

Neighbours   Nervous-system   Parochialism   Routine

Short-distances   Siblings   Speaking   Thinking   Tracks & Ways

Vehicles   Words (use of)   Writing

FOURTH HOUSE KEYWORD CLOUD

Ancestors Background Belonging Buildings Burial-place

Buried Devas DNA Dream-Life Mother-Earth-connection

Family Foundation(s) Gene-pool Ground(ing) Home

Inner-life Mines Nature Origins Parent (weaker) Private-life

Roots Security Subjectivity Personal-Unconscious

FIFTH HOUSE KEYWORD CLOUD

Affairs Children Creations Creativity Display Fun & Games

Gambling Hobbies Passions Pastimes Play Recreation

Romance Self-expression Sex Speculation Teaching

The-Stage Vacation

SIXTH HOUSE KEYWORD CLOUD

Agency Animals (small) Apprenticeship

Assimilation Bodymind Cleaning Clinical-Correctness

Coaching Co-workers Efficiency Employment Exactitude

Health (bodymind) Job Methods Pets Preparation

Psyche^Soma Service Sorting Training Welfare Work

Work-place

SEVENTH HOUSE KEYWORD CLOUD

Adversaries   Alter-ego   Balancing-factor   Better-half

Life-as-Mirror   Marriage   Opposition   Others   Partner

Projected-self   Public   Relationships   Shadow   Society

Strangers

EIGHTH HOUSE KEYWORD CLOUD

Business   Contracts   Crisis   Death   Divorce   Hidden

Inheritance   Inner-Dwelling-Being   Intimacy   Joint-ownership

Astral/Occult-realms   The-Other-Side   Other's-Worth

Property-of-others   Secrecy   Sex   Sexuality   Soul-realm   Taxes

Transformation   Union

NINTH HOUSE KEYWORD CLOUD

Adventure   Animals (large)   Beliefs   Culture   Divinity

Foreign-Affairs   Foreign-matters   Higher-Education

Higher-Ground   Image-of-God/Goddess   Law(s)

Long-distance-travel   Morality   Philosophy   Publishing   Religion

Ritual   Seeking

TENTH HOUSE KEYWORD CLOUD

Achievement   Authority   Career   Celebrity   Employer   Fame

Material-Success   Mission   Objectivity   Outer-life   Outer-world

Parent (dominant)   Position   Profession   Public-image   Public-life

Recognition   Reputation   Status   Superiors   State   The System

Vocation

ELEVENTH HOUSE KEYWORD CLOUD

Activism   Aspirations   Associates   Brotherhood   Civilization

Clubs   Community   Demographics   Friends   Goals   Groups

Hopes   Humanity   Ideals   Media   Movements   Networking

Politics   Principles   Revolution   Science   Sisterhood

Social-Values   Societies

TWELFTH HOUSE KEYWORD CLOUD

Ashram   Astral-Realm   Asylum   Behind-the-Scenes

Collective-Unconscious   Confinement   Conscience   Gestation

Hospital   Institutions   Karma   Karmic-Issues   Meditation

Mystical   Past-lives   Previous-existence   Prison   Quantum-Field

Retreat   Subconscious   Suppressed-Contents-of-the-Psyche

The-Source   Unlived-life   Unseen-Realm   Womb-life

Chart 'A' Explained

CHART 'A' is the version of a Birth Chart which is obtained FREE from my website, http://www.lynbirkbeck.com/instant reports.html

A Birth Chart is a picture of the Sun, Moon and Planets in the sky exactly as it appeared at the time and place of your birth. If your soul had a console, this is probably what would be in the middle of it! Below is described what this particular version of a Birth Chart, CHART 'A', is comprised of.

The Chart Wheel, the circular image on the top half of the page, needn't concern you too much right now as it is the information given below the Chart Wheel that most readily shows your data for *Dynamic Interactive Astrology – Level One*. However, if you wish to know what the Chart Wheel consists of – and ultimately you will need to – read the following description. If not, just skip over it to the heading: Below the Chart Wheel.

The horizontal line bisecting the Wheel is simply the Horizon – with the visible sky above it, and the non-visible sky beneath it. The left half is called the Ascendant (AS) – that is, where the Sun, Moon and Planets are seen to rise. The other, more or less vertical line with MC at the top is called the Meridian, the upper half is the Midheaven (MC).

The familiar twelve Signs of the Zodiac form an imaginary band encircling the Earth, and this is seen on the Chart as the Wheel itself. The Sun, Moon, Planets, Ascendant and Midheaven are positioned in the Signs they were in at the time of birth.

The Sign that the Sun is in is what you know as your Sun-Sign or Star-Sign. Each Sign has the quality of one of the four Elements:

Red = Fire = Intuition/Creative
Pale-Blue = Air = Thinking/Intellectual*

Blue = Water = Feeling/Empathetic

Green = Earth = Sensation/Practical

*Traditionally Yellow is the color for Air, but it is not very practical visually.

The circular area within the Zodiacal band is divided into twelve segments called Houses, marked as the spoke-like House Cusps, with numerals denoting the Houses themselves. The First House begins with your Ascendant, going in an anticlockwise direction, and ends with next spoke which is the cusp or the beginning of the 2nd House, and so on.

In the inner circle are seen various colored lines joining one Planet with another which are graphic depictions of what are called Aspects. We will look at these in *Dynamic Interactive Astrology – Level Two*. Aspects are determined by any two planets forming a particular angle at the center of the Chart, i.e. where you were born. However, one of the strongest aspects is the Conjunction. These, if you have any, are not marked by lines because they are made obvious by the Planets or Points involved being next door to one another.

Now that we have looked at the Chart Wheel itself, we will continue with how to easily read off the information you need to get quickly started with *Dynamic Interactive Astrology – Level One*.

Below the Chart Wheel – You will see the following information: Name of person whose chart it is; Date; Time; then Place of Birth with its Longitude and Latitude. Please check this information is correct.

The information given immediately below the name and birth data lists the Sun, Moon and Planets, Ascendant (or First House Cusp) and MC (Midheaven or 10th House Cusp) and finally the North Lunar Node, all with their glyphs, Sign glyphs, names of Sign positions and then their House placement numbers in the second to last column.

The last column gives positions by degree and minute of arc, but you may ignore these figures for the time being.

You will then see the Planet Aspect List. However reading off your Aspects will be explained in detail in *Dynamic Interactive Astrology – Level Two*.

O-BOOKS

SPIRITUALITY

O is a symbol of the world, of oneness and unity; this eye represents knowledge and insight. We publish titles on general spirituality and living a spiritual life. We aim to inform and help you on your own journey in this life.

If you have enjoyed this book, why not tell other readers by posting a review on your preferred book site?

Recent bestsellers from O-Books are:

Heart of Tantric Sex
Diana Richardson
Revealing Eastern secrets of deep love and intimacy to Western
couples.
Paperback: 978-1-90381-637-0 ebook: 978-1-84694-637-0

Crystal Prescriptions
The A-Z guide to over 1,200 symptoms and their healing crystals
Judy Hall
The first in the popular series of eight books, this handy little guide
is packed as tight as a pill-bottle with crystal remedies for ailments.
Paperback: 978-1-90504-740-6 ebook: 978-1-84694-629-5

Take Me To Truth
Undoing the Ego
Nouk Sanchez, Tomas Vieira
The best-selling step-by-step book on shedding the Ego, using the
teachings of *A Course In Miracles*.
Paperback: 978-1-84694-050-7 ebook: 978-1-84694-654-7

The 7 Myths about Love...Actually!
The Journey from your HEAD to the HEART of your SOUL
Mike George
Smashes all the myths about LOVE.
Paperback: 978-1-84694-288-4 ebook: 978-1-84694-682-0

The Holy Spirit's Interpretation of the New Testament
A Course in Understanding and Acceptance
Regina Dawn Akers
Following on from the strength of *A Course In Miracles*, NTI
teaches us how to experience the love and oneness of God.
Paperback: 978-1-84694-085-9 ebook: 978-1-78099-083-5

The Message of A Course In Miracles
A translation of the Text in plain language
Elizabeth A. Cronkhite
A translation of *A Course in Miracles* into plain, everyday
language for anyone seeking inner peace. The companion
volume, *Practicing A Course In Miracles*, offers practical lessons
and mentoring.
Paperback: 978-1-84694-319-5 ebook: 978-1-84694-642-4

Your Simple Path
Find Happiness in every step
Ian Tucker
A guide to helping us reconnect with what is really important in
our lives.
Paperback: 978-1-78279-349-6 ebook: 978-1-78279-348-9

365 Days of Wisdom
Daily Messages To Inspire You Through The Year
Dadi Janki
Daily messages which cool the mind, warm the heart and guide
you along your journey.
Paperback: 978-1-84694-863-3 ebook: 978-1-84694-864-0

Body of Wisdom
Women's Spiritual Power and How it Serves
Hilary Hart
Bringing together the dreams and experiences of women across
the world with today's most visionary spiritual teachers.
Paperback: 978-1-78099-696-7 ebook: 978-1-78099-695-0

Dying to Be Free
From Enforced Secrecy to Near Death to True Transformation
Hannah Robinson
After an unexpected accident and near-death experience, Hannah
Robinson found herself radically transforming her life, while a
remarkable new insight altered her relationship with her father, a
practising Catholic priest.
Paperback: 978-1-78535-254-6 ebook: 978-1-78535-255-3

The Ecology of the Soul
A Manual of Peace, Power and Personal Growth for Real People
in the Real World
Aidan Walker
Balance your own inner Ecology of the Soul to regain your
natural state of peace, power and wellbeing.
Paperback: 978-1-78279-850-7 ebook: 978-1-78279-849-1

Not I, Not other than I
The Life and Teachings of Russel Williams
Steve Taylor, Russel Williams
The miraculous life and inspiring teachings of one of the World's
greatest living Sages.
Paperback: 978-1-78279-729-6 ebook: 978-1-78279-728-9

On the Other Side of Love
A woman's unconventional journey towards wisdom
Muriel Maufroy
When life has lost all meaning, what do you do?
Paperback: 978-1-78535-281-2 ebook: 978-1-78535-282-9

Practicing A Course In Miracles
A translation of the Workbook in plain language, with
mentor's notes
Elizabeth A. Cronkhite
The practical second and third volumes of The Plain-Language
A Course In Miracles.
Paperback: 978-1-84694-403-1 ebook: 978-1-78099-072-9

Quantum Bliss
The Quantum Mechanics of Happiness, Abundance, and Health
George S. Mentz
Quantum Bliss is the breakthrough summary of success and
spirituality secrets that customers have been waiting for.
Paperback: 978-1-78535-203-4 ebook: 978-1-78535-204-1

The Upside Down Mountain
Mags MacKean
A must-read for anyone weary of chasing success and happiness
– one woman's inspirational journey swapping the uphill slog for
the downhill slope.
Paperback: 978-1-78535-171-6 ebook: 978-1-78535-172-3

Your Personal Tuning Fork
The Endocrine System
Deborah Bates
Discover your body's health secret, the endocrine system, and
'twang' your way to sustainable health!
Paperback: 978-1-84694-503-8 ebook: 978-1-78099-697-4

Readers of ebooks can buy or view any of these bestsellers by clicking on the live link in the title. Most titles are published in paperback and as an ebook. Paperbacks are available in traditional bookshops. Both print and ebook formats are available online.

Find more titles and sign up to our readers' newsletter at http://www.johnhuntpublishing.com/mind-body-spirit

Follow us on Facebook at https://www.facebook.com/OBooks/ and Twitter at https://twitter.com/obooks